What is going on in

Christian

Sex Education?

_____

ES Williams

What is going on in Christian Sex Education? is published by
Belmont House Publishing

First published October 2009

ISBN 0 9548493 3 7

Unless otherwise stated, biblical quotations are taken from the
New King James Version of the Holy Bible © 1994 by Thomas
Nelson, Inc. Used by permission

Published by Belmont House Publishing
36 The Crescent
Belmont
SUTTON
Surrey SM2 6BJ

Website www.belmonthouse.co.uk

Cover designed by Adam Shah

A catalogue record for this book is available from the British
Library

Printed by Cromwell Press Group

Contents

List of illustrations

Preface

Sex education has proved to be a difficult issue for the Christian Church. In 1974 the British Government, by an Act of Parliament, became responsible for supplying children of any age, even children as young as 11 or 12, with free contraception, without the knowledge or consent of their parents. The claim was that contraception would protect young people from unwanted pregnancies and sexually transmitted diseases. As a consequence vast numbers of children and young people now have ready access to contraceptives.

Sex education has been the vehicle for teaching children how to access and use contraception and has been very successful in achieving this aim. Many local health services across the UK are encouraging schoolchildren to register with a school nurse so that they can collect a free supply of condoms – no questions asked. However, stories in the popular press of under-aged children being given contraceptives, or even an abortion, behind their parents' back have caused a sense of unease among the general population. How can such things be happening in the UK?

Despite the explicit nature of the sex education that is being delivered in the school classroom, and a large increase in sexual promiscuity among children, there has been little response from the Church. Many Christians, because of the controversial nature of the subject, would rather leave it to the so-called experts in sex education.

In my role as a professional in public health, and with a background in clinical medicine, I have been in a position to see the consequences of the Government's policy at first hand. My research into sex education, published in *Lessons in Depravity* (2003), uncovered the amoral ideology that drives the sex education industry. During my research I was disturbed to find that the sex education programmes of a number of Christian organisations were deeply compromised.

My warning to this effect, carefully documented in *Lessons in Depravity* and the *Outrage of Amoral Sex Education* (2006) proved to be unpopular, and both books were negatively reviewed in *Evangelicals Now*. According to one reviewer: 'Dr Williams attacks his fellow Christians with the same apparent ease that he berates the sexual revolutionaries.' Yet no attempt has been made to answer the serious issues that have been raised.

It is no surprise, then, that the Christian version of sex education, led by CARE, a mainline Christian charity, has continued to flourish. CARE's vision is that its new sex education programme, entitled *evaluate... informing choice*, should be available to every school across England, Scotland and Wales. Many churches support CARE's ministry and teams of Christians, mainly women, are being trained to deliver the *evaluate* sex education programme. The purpose of this book is to draw attention to what is being done in the name of the Christian faith and with Christian money.

ES Williams, October 2009

Acronyms and Initialisms

ABC sex education   Abstain, Be faithful, Condoms

Brook   Brook Advisory Centres

BPAS   British Pregnancy Advisory Service

CARE   Christian Action Research and Education

CMF   Christian Medical Fellowship

FPA or fpa   Family Planning Association

IPPF   International Planned Parenthood Federation

IUD   intra-uterine device

NHS   National Health Service

PCT   Primary Care Trust

SRE   Sex and relationship education

STIs   sexually transmitted infections

STDs   sexually transmitted diseases

WHO   World Health Organisation

With thanks to John Turner and Graham Parkhouse for their advice and encouragement, and to Adam Shah for designing the cover and helping with the graphics.

1

The sex education controversy

Sex education remains a highly controversial subject that raises strong feelings. On one side are those who believe that the answer to the widely publicised crisis in teenage pregnancies lies in providing children with clear guidance on contraception so that they know how to 'protect' themselves. They see sex education as a human right, claiming that young people need information to make informed, healthy choices about their sexual options. On the other side are those who are highly critical of sex education, arguing that it is not only ineffective in preventing teenage pregnancies, but that it encourages sexual promiscuity. They believe that sexual conduct falls within a moral framework that should be addressed solely within the family, for it is the responsibility of parents to use Scripture to guide their children in the area of sexual conduct. This controversy has raged over the last three decades.

Media coverage of sex education

Adding fuel to the controversy is the fact that sex education receives wide coverage in the popular press and on TV. An article in *The Daily Telegraph* under the headline, 'Outrage over explicit sex lessons', made the point that the use of crude and explicit sex education materials is widespread in schools. John Clare, *The Telegraph's* education correspondent, describes how parents are kept in the dark about what is being taught in the school classroom. 'No issue I have raised in the Any Questions column over the past nine years has angered so many readers quite as much as last week's item on 12-year-olds being taught about anal, oral and digital sex. Parents and grandparents wrote in droves to say how horrified, appalled, disgusted and outraged they were.'[1]

The *Manchester Evening News,* under the headline 'Outrage at bid to sell condoms in schools', tells of a plan to sell condoms in school tuck shops. Those promoting the idea apparently believe that making cut-price contraceptives available in school shops and vending machines would dramatically reduce teenage pregnancies. Nick Seaton, chairman of the Campaign for Real Education, responded in robust fashion, 'I don't think any parent would think condoms should be sold on school premises at all. Children go to school to learn English, maths, science, geography and so on – not to learn about sex. I think most parents will be horrified.'[2]

In response to the headline 'Doctors paid to give contraceptive injection to teenage girls', Norman Wells of Family and Youth Concern, responded, 'Parents of girls under 16 will be alarmed to think that doctors are going to be given financial incentives to provide their daughters with contraception behind their backs. It is tantamount to bribing doctors to facilitate under-age sex. The more the Government has invested in schemes to promote contraception among teenagers, the more young people have become sexually active and the higher rates of sexually transmitted infection have risen.'[3]

A pilot scheme in six schools across Oxfordshire encourages 11-year-olds to ask for the morning-after pill via a text message so that they are not embarrassed into admitting that they are having sex. The scheme was condemned by Dr Andrew Fergusson of the Christian Medical Fellowship, 'Sexual intercourse at the age of 11 is a criminal offence and the local authorities should not turn a blind eye. The idea of removing all face-to-face contact with a health professional is another sign of the trivialization of sexual intercourse and the breakdown of trust between young people and adults.'[4]

A front page news item, 'Abortion Ads on Television', tells of a proposal to allow condom manufacturers to advertise their products at any time of the day or night. This will mean that Britain has one of the most liberal broadcasting regimes in the world. The Broadcast Committee on Advertising Practice says that it is responding to the Government's call for action to combat rising rates of teenage pregnancy. Dr Peter Saunders of the Christian Medical Fellowship responded, 'The problem is that the Government's strategy on teenage pregnancy, based on condoms, the morning-after pill and abortion has failed.'[5]

A primary school in Devon was forced to reconsider its sex education policy after parents complained of an offensive film to be shown to children as young as five. Parents said the DVD and accompanying worksheets were far too graphic for impressionable children. The controversial *Living and Growing* material, commissioned by Channel 4, features illustrations of a naked man and woman and invites youngsters to label the genitalia. One concerned parent who has a five-year-old daughter at the school said: 'I find it offensive. The programme is inappropriate and unsuitable for a five or six-year-old. I think the school has made a grave error of judgement which is morally wrong. We were told it was part of a programme to reduce teenage pregnancies in Torbay. Teaching my daughter about her private parts is not going to stop teenage pregnancies. It's liberal clap-trap.'[6]

The Department for Children, Schools and Families is working with the Brook Advisory Centres (an organisation that specialises in providing contraceptive services for under-age children) to develop a national condom card scheme for boys. Condom 'credit cards', also known as C-cards, allow boys as young as 13 to pick up a free supply of condoms at football grounds, barber shops and scout huts. The idea is for condoms to be made readily available at places where boys congregate, in order to spare them the embarrassment of visiting a sexual health clinic or GP surgery or facing a shop assistant.

According to new government guidance the C-card will be issued after a boy has attended a safe-sex lesson. Those who take advantage of the scheme will not have to give their names or answer questions about their sex lives and parents will not be told. The C-card scheme, which is already used by some local authorities, will be made available to all 13-year-olds in Britain when the guidance is published in the autumn of 2009. Moreover, councils will have discretion to offer C-cards to sexually active boys of 11 or 12. Simon Blake, chief executive of Brook, said the C-card would make condom use 'an everyday reality'.[7]

The controversy

Even among those in favour of sex education there is a divergence of opinion over what should be taught. On the one side are those who support what has become known as comprehensive sex education and on the other side those who support an approach that focuses on abstinence.

Comprehensive sex education

Most supporters of comprehensive sex education regard the decision of teenagers to become sexually active as a matter of personal choice that should not be dictated by religious or political dogmas. They believe that to be truly effective, sex education must give children all the facts of life so that they can make an informed decision about their sexual conduct. Access to information about sex, contraception and sexually transmitted infections (STIs) is regarded as a human right—young people need information in order to make choices about the best way of protecting themselves against the risks of 'unprotected' sex. They claim that moralising about sexual conduct is not only unhelpful, but may be positively harmful.

Supporters of comprehensive sex education criticise abstinence programmes as being ineffective, causing confusion in the minds of young people. The Sex Education Forum, an umbrella body that brings together a range of organisations involved in sex education, having undertaken a review of abstinence programmes in the USA, produced the report *Just Say No! to Abstinence Education* (2001). The authors argue that these programmes use fear tactics to promote the ideal of abstinence and usually omit discussion of topics like abortion and homosexuality, or present them as morally wrong. They are concerned that most abstinence programmes do not provide information on contraception other than failure rates which are exaggerated. Brook believes that 'teaching abstinence alone denies young people access to impartial and accurate information which they need to make informed choices and to protect their sexual health'. They claim that comprehensive sex education, combined with access to confidential contraceptive services, helps young people to delay becoming sexually active.[8]

The sex education strategy of the Government is based on the comprehensive approach. Other organisations that promote comprehensive sex education include the Family Planning Association and Brook.

Abstinence education

Abstinence sex education has been developed in the USA by programmes such as Project Reality, True Love Waits and the Silver Ring Thing. The aim of these programmes is to teach young people that they should make a commitment to abstain from sex until marriage. The Silver Ring Thing has gained international recognition for its lively shows aimed at young people that feature music, laser lights and comedy performances. Young people are encouraged to make a vow of abstinence and sign a pledge card. In 1995 a new event was created that used rings instead of cards as a visible reminder of the abstinence pledge.

Many supporters of the abstinence approach come to the issue from a religious or moral point of view, arguing that a clear message to abstain from sex is central. They are concerned that discussions of sex and contraception may encourage early and potentially unsafe sexual behaviour. Some supporters take a pragmatic approach, arguing that abstinence is a sensible, healthy choice. In the UK abstinence education has no support in public policy and receives no funding from government.

ABC sex education or Abstinence plus

A third position, known as the ABC approach (A for Abstain, B for Be faithful and C for Condoms), which is really a compromise between the two positions mentioned above, is gaining wide support as many organisations are now seeking for an accommodation that allows a unified approach to what they call 'sexual health prevention' strategies. ABC sex education is also referred to as abstinence plus because condoms are added as an option.

An article in *The Lancet* (November 2004), the prestigious medical journal, signed by nearly 150 experts from around the world, including many Christian organisations, has led the way by calling for consensus around the ABC approach to prevention. The article, which acknowledges the tension between comprehensive and abstinence sex education, concludes that 'the time has come to leave behind divisive polarisation and to move forward together in designing and implementing evidence-based prevention programmes to help reduce the millions of new infections occurring each year'.[9] This consensus around ABC has opened the way for Christians to join with secular organisations in constructing and delivering sex education programmes.

The ABC approach is now at the centre of the HIV/AIDS prevention strategy of the World Health Organisation (WHO).[10] Many secular organisations, including Marie Stopes International (Uganda), are passionate supporters of the ABC approach. Their leaflet, *Life is precious... guard it well*, advises a young person, 'You still have a long life ahead of you and you will want to keep it that way. HIV/AIDS is preventable, so avoid the virus by thinking carefully before you have sex and choose from ABC.' The leaflet explains the ABC approach:

> A – Abstain from sex altogether. If you don't have sex, you don't take a risk. This is the only way to ensure that you don't get HIV/AIDS and other sexually transmitted infections – it's 100% effective.

> B – Be faithful to one uninfected partner. If you and your partner have protected yourselves in the past, and stick with each other in the future without taking other partners, you can avoid the risk of HIV/AIDS and other sexually transmitted infections.

> C – If you cannot be sure of your partner's sexual behaviour either now or in the past, and you want to have sex, then you need to use a condom.

If you choose to have sex, you can avoid the risk of contracting HIV/AIDS and other sexually transmitted infections by using condoms. It's your future… make your choice.

Dr Trevor Stammers, chairman of the Christian Medical Fellowship (CMF)

Why ABC?

A Abstain from sex altogether. If you don't have sex, you don't take a risk. This is the only way to ensure that you don't get HIV/AIDS and other sexually transmitted infections - it's 100% effective!

B - Be faithful to one uninfected partner. If you and your partner have protected yourselves in the past, and stick with each other in the future without taking other partners, you can avoid the risk of HIV/AIDS and other sexually transmitted infections.

C - If you cannot be sure of your partner's sexual behaviour either now or in the past, and you want to have sex, then you need to use a condom.

Life is precious – Marie Stopes International (Uganda)

and a prominent commentator on sex education, recognises the benefits of the ABC approach. 'What the ABC success teaches is that a range of options is now needed in the UK to help teenagers to defer sexual intercourse until they are in a secure, committed and loving relationship; to encourage faithfulness and partner reduction among the sexually active – and to promote condom use among those who engage in higher risk sex.'[11] The CMF is in the forefront of a campaign to persuade the British Government to adopt the ABC approach. According to the General Secretary, Dr Peter Saunders, 'The Government has persistently clung to promoting condoms as the main plank of its policy to counter the highest rates of teenage STIs in Europe, when what is really needed are policies aimed at behaviour change. The best way to counter this epidemic effectively is to promote real behaviour change through such programmes as the very successful ABC (Abstain, Be faithful, Condoms) programme in Uganda or the Love for Life programme in Northern Ireland.'[12] The CMF claims that the ABC model is based on biblical principles.[13]

Oasis Esteem is a Christian charity founded by Steve Chalke that teaches the ABC model of sex education in secondary schools. The head of Oasis Esteem says that their sex educators have found that the message of abstinence – 'you don't have to have sex'; 'it's okay to wait'; 'not everyone is doing it' – is actually very liberating for young people facing peer pressure to become sexually active. However, teaching young people solely about the benefits of choosing abstinence and delaying sex is not considered to be complete sex education. 'With this in mind, Oasis Esteem has decided to adopt the ABC model, which teaches the benefits of sexual abstinence, be faithful to your partner and condom use for those sexually active with more than one partner. It is the approach favoured by the World Health Organisation and credited with reducing HIV/AIDS infection rates in countries like Uganda.'[14]

So the ABC approach to sex education, recommended by the WHO, is propagated by Marie Stopes International, the Christian Medical Fellowship, Oasis Esteem and, as we shall see in chapter 5, by CARE.

Dr Chris Richards, the founder of Lovewise, has challenged the morality of ABC sex education. 'At first sight there is a logical and emotional appeal in combining the promotion of sexual abstinence to everyone with the safety net of the condom to those who won't abstain. This is known as the 'abstinence plus' approach in the US. However, condom promotion to the unmarried in an amoral context is always wrong… Also, inevitably abstinence and safer sex messages contradict each other. For example, abstinence education is aspiring them to purity and self-control whereas a safer sex message anticipates and therefore affirms a lack of both (except, inconsistently, in the self-control needed to put the condom on in the heat of the moment).'[15]

Richards is correct in pointing to the moral contradictions that underpin the ABC approach and which undermine biblical teaching on the subject. It follows that the CMF is wrong to claim that it is based on biblical principles. ABC sex education simply provides young people with a sexual menu from which to select the option that most satisfies their sexual needs. It is a misplaced attempt to find a compromise between two fundamentally opposed views of sexual conduct. The biblical view is discussed in chapter 4.

A biblical approach to sexual conduct

The only Christian organisation in the UK that teaches about sexual conduct from Scripture, to my knowledge, is Lovewise, a Christian charity that was started by two Newcastle paediatricians in 2002, Dr Chris Richards and Dr Liz Jones. Chris Richards explains the motivation for setting up Lovewise. '[We] have become increasingly aware in our Newcastle clinics and schools of how much our young people are suffering from the consequences of sex outside marriage and the disintegration of home life. We believe that safe(r) sex teaching has contributed to this by promoting sex at a younger age and outside a moral framework. Our desire is to see this ungodly teaching replaced by one from a Christian perspective in order to help rebuild the family in our society.'[16]

Lovewise acknowledges that 'ideally intimate issues of sexuality should be modelled and taught by a child's parents'. However, because of the decline in society many children are in need of moral guidance. 'We have thought long and hard about exactly how we should present a godly perspective on relationships.' Themes discussed cover all aspects of God's word – his creation, moral law, judgement and grace.

Lovewise produces a range of presentations for use by schools and churches. The presentations use personal testimonies, medical facts and common sense arguments, all underpinned by biblical principles, to teach about the God-given boundaries for sex and encourage pupils to aspire to marriage and parenthood. 'We explain the superior nature of marriage compared to living together in terms of duration, fidelity and children's upbringing. Rather than the safe(r) sex perspective of pregnancy avoidance, we explain the great privilege of sharing in the creation of new life and the joy of parenthood in marriage.' The consequences of sex outside of marriage are considered, and the failure rate of condoms explained.

The pupils are also given help on how to avoid sexual intimacy whilst going out. This includes the need for self-control, the dangers of alcohol and provocation through dress, behaviour and pornography. Most importantly, especially since some pupils are likely to have already been sexually active, they are told of the hope of forgiveness for past mistakes. Dr Richards comments, 'Many teachers thank us for teaching what they know is true but fear to teach themselves in the current philosophical climate. We give the presentations in faith remembering the power of God's word and the Lord's reminder of the harvest from seed that we scatter, which grows night and day independent of us!'[17]

Other Lovewise resources include a powerpoint presentation 'Growing up – growing wise@home' that helps parents to provide God-honouring teaching about marriage and relationships that is appropriate to the child's age, and a booklet *Going Out, Marriage and Sex – what the Bible says about it* (2005) which provides young people with biblical advice on relationships.

The Lovewise initiative is important for it shows that it is possible for Christians to be faithful to biblical teaching and yet gain access to the school classroom.

The Christian response

Despite the encouraging ministry of Lovewise, many churches are unsure how they should respond to the sex education agenda and would rather not be involved for the subject is regarded as too controversial. As a consequence most Christian parents have little idea what their children are being taught. While some don't like what they hear about sex education they are reluctant to speak out for fear of being seen as narrow minded moralizers. Others believe that children need sex education and so the challenge is to find a sensitive 'Christian' version. Those who support this view argue that it is not good enough for Christians simply to criticise the sex education that is being delivered by the Government—we need to come forward with a positive alternative.

The purpose of this book is to describe the version of sex education developed by CARE (Christian Action Research and Education) a large well funded Christian charity that receives financial and prayer support from many evangelical churches.

(Endnotes)

1 *The Daily Telegraph*, 23 November 2005, Outrage over explicit sex lessons, John Clare
2 *Manchester Evening News*, 5 May 2004, Outrage at bid to sell condoms in schools, Deborah Haile
3 *The Daily Telegraph*, 13 February 2009, Doctors paid to give contraceptive injection to teenage girls
4 *The Daily Telegrap*h, 25 March 2009, Schoolgirls text for morning after pill, Caroline Gammell
5 *Daily Mail*, 26 March 2009, Abortion Ads on Television, Sean Poulter
6 *Mail Online*, 26 February 2007, Outcry over explicit sex education video shown to five-year-olds, Luke Salfeld
7 *The Sunday Times*, June 7 2009, Boys to get credit card for condoms, Marie Woolf, Whitehall Editor
8 Brook Advisory Centres website, Policy and research, Brook's position on abstinence education
9 Halperin DJ et al., The time has come for common ground on preventing sexual transmission of HIV, *The Lancet*, 27 November 2004, 364, pp1913–4
10 WHO position statement on condoms, Condoms and HIV Prevention, July 2004
11 TG Stammers, As easy as ABC? Primary prevention of sexually transmitted infections, editorial, *Post Graduate Medical Journal*, 2005, vol. pp 273– 275
12 Christian Medical Fellowship, press release, 20 May 2005, Teenage sexual health – abandon your ambulance at the bottom of the cliff policies, CMF tells government
13 *Triple Helix*, The AIDS pandemic, Peter Saunders, Winter 2004
14 *Guardian Unlimited*, 21 September 2005, Breaking the taboo, Catriona Martin
15 Chris Richards, Sex education in schools, *Nucleus*, July 2005
16 Chris Richards, Ibid
17 Chris Richards, Ibid

2

CARE enters the sex education arena

CARE evolved out of the National Festival of Light, a popular movement that developed in response to the permissive society of the 1960s. The Festival had two expressed aims—to protest against sex exploitation in the media and to offer the teaching of Christ as the key to recovering moral stability in the nation. An initial rally was held in early September 1971 in Westminster Central Hall, where the exploitation of sex and violence in the entertainment industry was denounced. The meeting was invaded by the Gay Liberation Front who sounded horns and turned off the lights, while the audience responded by singing hymns.

The Festival held more than seventy regional rallies around the UK. In Bristol the cathedral was filled to capacity, largely in reaction to the opening of a sex supermarket in the city. A nationwide day of prayer was observed in mid September and on the night of the twenty-third bonfires and torches were lit on hilltops throughout Britain. There were about 300 such beacons, with 100,000 people taking part in local events.

Two days later in Trafalgar Square the Festival reached its climax when around 35,000 people gathered, many having travelled by coach from distant parts of the country to hear more than a dozen speakers, among them Malcolm Muggeridge and Mary Whitehouse, call for a halt to the commercial exploitation of sex and violence. The message was that the values of love and respect for the individual and the family were under serious threat, and that once these were overthrown a stable society could not survive. The same message was proclaimed later that day at an open-air concert of Christian music in Hyde Park. Among the performers were Cliff Richard and Graham Kendrick. Other open-air music festivals were held, such as the London Festival for Jesus, which offered teaching on Christian lifestyle and gospel outreach.

After the excitement of the Festival the leadership committee continued to meet and in 1983 Lyndon Bowring and Charlie Colchester and others formally established the ministry of CARE. The high-profile style of the Festival gave way to a more discreet range of initiatives that aimed to help people who were suffering as a consequence of the social breakdown in British society. CARE also believed that it should take a Christian stand on political and moral issues.

CARE's vision 'is to see the transformation of society into one that has a greater respect for the sanctity and value of human life from fertilisation to its natural end'.[1] It claims to be working towards a society that honours the family as the foundation of a stable society. CARE's prayer guide (April to August 2007) reminds supporters of its important ministry in the fields of pregnancy counselling and sex education:

> Prayer is a top priority for us at CARE. From the beginning of our ministry in the 1970s, a monthly list of requests was distributed to the handful of supporters who shared our desire to make a Christian difference in society. Over the years this simple intercessory tool has evolved to become today's Prayer Guide, which aims to inform and inspire Christians to pray about a wide range of issues...
>
> With the backing of our 100,000 supporters, CARE is:
>
> • involved in the political arena and the media
>
> • supporting 160 Christian crisis pregnancy centres and a free phone helpline
>
> • running an innovative schools sex and relationships education initiative...[2]

CARE's commitment to human rights

Over the years CARE has sought to bring Christian insight and experience to matters of public policy and to engage 'with the political process in regards to equality issues, particularly issues of religious freedom and human rights'.[3] CARE's Institute for Faith & Culture aims to equip Christian graduates with the tools they need to engage effectively within a secular culture.

CARE has a seat on the Religion and Belief Consultative Group on equality and diversity, which advises the new Equality and Human Rights Commission.[4] (The Commission came into being in October 2007. It combines the responsibilities and powers of the three previous equality commissions. Its main purpose is to promote and protect human rights in the UK). Other members of the Consultative Group are the Inter Faith Network, Faithworks, the Evangelical Alliance, the British Humanist Association and the National Secular Society.[5]

In October 2008, CARE welcomed over a hundred guests to the Houses of Parliament to commemorate the sixtieth anniversary of the Universal Declaration of Human Rights. Nola Leach, CARE's chief executive, in her welcome speech stressed the importance of the Declaration. 'This, the greatest of the human rights documents, emerged from the ruins of the Second World War in the autumn of 1948 and is a testimony to the success of the negotiators in agreeing a common set of universal principles that cross all cultures, religions and political systems... Rather than pursuing more and more rights, we must use the opportunity of the sixtieth anniversary to celebrate and remind ourselves of the vital importance of the Universal Declaration.' She went on to say that the Universal Declaration remains a vital tool that has shaped lives across the globe—it is so foundational that it has been described as a 'Magna Carta for all humanity'.[6]

On the tenth of December 2008 CARE marked the anniversary of the Universal Declaration of Human Rights at a lunch for ambassadors in the United Nations Headquarters on 1st Avenue, New York. According to CARE's International Director Charlie Hoare, the United Nations events were important in demonstrating CARE's commitment to universal human rights. He said, 'We will continue to work in partnership with member states and the UN's Human Rights Council to promote the dignity of all human beings around the world.'[7]

CARE's commitment to sex education

CARE entered the sex education arena in the early 1990s. The argument was that as sex education was here to stay the Christian Church needed to become involved. CARE's report *Your School and Sex Education* (1996) provided guidance on how to produce a sex education policy. CARE claimed that although there is a debate in society as to the best methods of reducing teenage pregnancies, as well as ways to reduce under-age sexual activity, 'there is no doubt that schools are recognised as having a part to play. Sex education is not an issue that can be ignored!'[8] The report was revised and published as *Sex and Relationship Education* (2001).[9] Under the heading useful websites, the report gives the web address of the Sex Education Forum.

Make Love Last

One of CARE's early initiatives was the video *Make Love Last*, produced in 1994, with the message that it's okay to say 'no' to sex. I first came across this video when I was Director of Public Health for Croydon Health Authority and closely involved with policy on health promotion and sex education. It was a relief when two Christian colleagues informed me of a video that was being developed by CARE that would teach about sexual conduct from a Christian perspective. We saw CARE's involvement in sex education as a beacon of hope in an otherwise bleak situation, for most Christians working in health and education were extremely concerned with the amoral tone and explicit nature of the sex education that was being taught to schoolchildren.

As I became increasingly engaged in the sex education agenda I decided to investigate the issue from a Christian viewpoint. The result of my research was *Lessons in Depravity* (2003), a book which demonstrates the link between the ideology of the sexual revolution and sex education. I spent three years researching the subject, examining a wide range of materials in detail, and it was during this time that I first viewed CARE's video *Make Love Last*. I was concerned to see that the video was partly funded by the Department of Health, for the danger was that having taken Government money, CARE was promoting a message that was consistent with the Government's sex education strategy. It would be an understatement to say that I was disturbed by what I saw. The whole tone and presentation of the video was to trivialize sex, even referring to one character as Randy Factor. Moreover, there was no Christian teaching and almost no difference from the messages that were being propagated by the sex education programmes of organisations such as the FPA, the Health Promotion Agency and Brook. Here is a summary of what I wrote in *Lessons in Depravity*:

> CARE's video *Make Love Last* purports to be a video that delivers a sex education message to young people from a Christian perspective... The video contains many smutty sexual innuendoes. One character, Randy Factor, asks a group of young people whether they are 'putting it around a bit, you know, dipping your wick'. Randy promotes an exercise programme to make people 'bonking' fit. He uses phrases like, 'You need to get bonking fit'; 'pumping for humping'; 'leg-over time'; 'the more I score the better I score' and 'the sponsored bonk'. A dictionary defines most of these phrases as 'coarse slang' for having sexual intercourse. In a 'stud of the month' competition Randy gets a young man to admit that, in his dreams, he had impregnated the entire female staff of a nightclub between two and four in the morning. In a skit on the TV programme Blind Date, Randy has his game-show called Find a Mate. The young male contestant explains to the first female that strip poker is his favourite game and asks her: 'Will you go all the way when I let you play with me?' He asks the second young woman: 'Will you let me touch you up, or should I use a stripper?' His question to the third woman is even more direct: 'Will you have sex with me?' The prize is a dirty weekend in Paris, staying at Bonking Motel. It is surprising that CARE thinks it is necessary to use this type of language to deliver a message to young people. Surely it must know that the Bible warns against obscenity, foolish talk and coarse joking? (Ephesians 5:4).

> And CARE is apparently content for its message on sexual behaviour to be associated with the magazine *Just 17*, widely known for its salacious sexual outlook.[10]

Having studied the biblical view of sexual conduct, which emphasises the virtues of chastity, modesty and self-control (see chapter 4), it was clear to me that the message of *Make Love Last* had nothing to do with the Christian faith. It was at this point that I realized that I needed to study CARE's sex education programme in more detail. Was *Make Love Last* just an aberration or did it represent CARE's approach? What follows in this book is the result of my research. I believe that it is important for the Church to understand what is being done in its name.

Parents First

In 1995, CARE produced *Parents First – Sex Education within the Home* as a training manual for churches. Lyndon Bowring encourages 'church leaders to consider incorporating *Parents First* into their teaching programme. I know that parents will be very grateful to you for tackling these rarely discussed issues so directly.'[11] Among the authors are Ann Holt, Director of CARE for Education, Angela Flux, an experienced educator who helped develop the video *Make Love Last*, and Dr Trevor Stammers.

The *Parents First* programme claims to help parents tackle sex education confidently and appropriately with their children. The manual warns that while 'the material is firmly based on Christian teaching', the course leader 'may encounter embarrassment, even hostility at first and this needs to be anticipated and worked through'.[12] But why would material that is firmly based on Christian teaching produce embarrassment and hostility among Christian parents?

Parents First provides a broad range of activities to guide parents on how to talk to their children about sex, and challenges the notion that 'talking about sex and sexuality to younger children is somehow wrong and robs them of their innocence'. Nonsense, says CARE. 'If we talk about sexuality as a natural, normal part of life, our children will accept it as a natural, normal part of life. If it takes place in our conversation as something we are happy to talk about appropriately, then it will not be flagged up as some mysterious subject likely to create far more interest to a curious child… early childhood offers all sorts of situations where sexuality can be discussed: bath time, birth of younger siblings, observing a breast-feeding Mum, learning the names of the sexual organs, toilet training, appropriate and inappropriate affection/touching and so on.'[13]

What is so disturbing about this guidance is that it takes no account of the natural innocence of childhood. Scripture never instructs parents to talk to their children about sex—indeed, Scripture does not use the word. Every reference to sexual activity in the Bible is made in euphemistic terms. 'Now Adam knew Eve his wife, and she conceived and bore Cain' (Genesis 4:1). The sexual organs – our unpresentable parts – are to have greater modesty (1 Corinthians 12:23). It is the sex educators that openly talk about sex, not the people of God.

Parents First claims that discussions around sexual language are very important. An activity sheet is handed out which requires parents to categorise a list of sexual words into polite, neutral, clinical and rude/offensive. For example, the words for sex are, sleep with; making love; sexual intercourse and screwing (see picture below). Other words on the activity sheet are penis, female genitalia, and oral sex for which parents are required to fill in the rude/offensive words. Parents are told that they will not have to show their completed activity sheet to anyone else or

---

Parents First

Activity 6

SEXUAL LANGUAGE

	'Polite' word/ inoffensive	Neutral / inoffensive	Clinical	Rude / Offensive
Female genitalia				
Penis				
Sex	Sleep with	Making love	Sexual intercourse	Screwing
Oral sex				

Parents First – Sex education within the home
CARE's manual for course leaders (page 36)

---

share their words with the group. If the 'group is quite comfortable with sexual language, the words can be anonymously collated onto a flip chart and used to illustrate the discussion on appropriate sexual language'.

The discussion that follows focuses on how the rude/offensive words make them feel, 'the importance of working out what type of language children should use' and 'the importance of parents and children being familiar with sexual language other than the "proper" word, to avoid innocent mistakes'.[14]

Apparently CARE feels that it is 'important' for Christians to have a vocabulary of lewd words in order to avoid innocent 'mistakes'. But why does this information need to be collated anonymously? Is it because the offensive words that this exercise is intended to generate might arouse a sense of shame in the mind of a Christian? Scripture instructs God's people not to let filthy language come from our mouths (Colossians 3:8). Christians must use 'wholesome words, even the words of our Lord Jesus Christ' (1 Timothy 6:3).

CARE responds to the Government's social exclusion unit

In 1998 CARE responded to a questionnaire from the Government's social exclusion unit on the issue of teenage parenthood. CARE's chief concern was that few people are asking the question, 'Whether it is healthy for teenagers to be having sex?'[15] CARE urges 'that accurate factual information is given to young people about sex, unplanned pregnancy, STIs, contraception, abortion, and its effects, both physical and emotional. We also support programmes that include self-awareness, self-image, decision-making, and promote emotional literacy.'[16]

CARE expresses the view that 'appropriate sex education can take place at school from age 5'.[17] 'Clear, unembarrassed appropriate early sex education provides a good foundation for more detail at secondary school age... Older children can learn more explicit details about sex in the context of loving relationships, with as much emphasis placed on the emotional aspects of teenage sex, pregnancy and abortion, as well as the physical.'[18] CARE acknowledges that 'there may be some aspects of sex education where pupils will appreciate being able to talk to adults who are not their teachers'.[19] However, it is not clear what adults it has in mind.

Quite a Catch

The leaflet, *Quite a Catch*, is important for it reveals the authority that underpins CARE's advice on sexual conduct. According to the leaflet:

> The World Health Organisation has stated that the best way to avoid becoming infected with an STI is to stay faithful to an uninfected partner for life. Delaying becoming sexually active is a positive health choice. Having fewer sexual partners reduces the risk of infection. Using a condom correctly every time means that you are less likely to get an STI but it is not 100% safe. Whether you've had sex or not, you have a choice about your sexual health. It affects your whole person, not just your body. Take care of yourself. [20]

Here we see the first example of CARE promoting the WHO's policy on sexual conduct. The purpose of *Quite a Catch* is to give young people a few pragmatic tips for avoiding STIs. The leaflet does not refer to Scripture, and there is nothing in the advice from the WHO to indicate that sexual activity outside marriage is wrong; there is no warning of the moral consequences of sexual sin. The advice of CARE's leaflet is, in fact, without moral content.

Evaluate... informing choice

CARE's latest venture into sex education, which was launched in 2003, is a programme entitled e*valuate... informing choice*. Lyndon Bowring, writing in his newsletter (June 2004), says that CARE's new sex education programme encourages healthy sexual choices and the delaying of sexual activity. CARE's *evaluate* website informs young people that 'If it's sex education you are looking for, then welcome to the website of e*valuate... informing choice*, a new Sex & Relationship Education programme designed with young people in mind. Colourful and dynamic, the set of three multimedia presentations are delivered in schools and youth settings by trained *evaluate* teams, who see the active involvement and engagement of their audience as vitally important in helping young people reach their full potential. Bringing a fresh, modern and direct edge to Sex & Relationship Education and lifestyle choices, *evaluate* teams empower young people to make healthy informed decisions and support them in delaying sexual experience until a long-term committed exclusive relationship.'[21]

CARE claims that *evaluate* presentations 'bring Christian values into today's youth culture in a non-threatening, non-preachy way. This programme has at its heart the underlying belief that every young person is a unique and valuable individual, capable of making and maintaining healthy choices if suitably equipped and supported.'[22]

CARE's vision is for *evaluate* to be available to every school across England, Scotland and Wales. Project officer Sue Lindars says that although the *evaluate* programme is not *overtly* Christian, she believes God has a plan. She said, 'God's heart aches for young people. We're confident that He is working through this project, intervening in a tragic situation.'[23] Here we should note that CARE concedes that its sex education programme is not *overtly* Christian. Apparently CARE believes that God is working *covertly* to get his message across to young people.

In *CARE Today* (2006 Winter) Sue Lindars expresses her delight with the way *evaluate* has developed since its launch. 'People are catching the vision. It seems we're coming into a new era. At the last conference, delegates were encouraging about the training. They seemed impressed

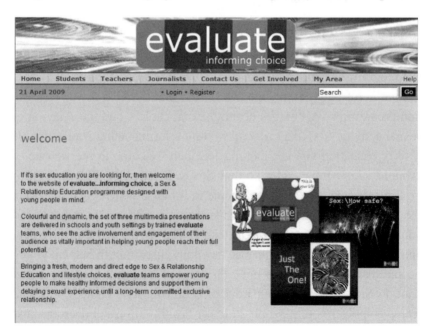

with the quality and professionalism. But they also feel that they are part of what God is doing to change young people's lives – and the way society thinks about sexuality.'[24]

According to CARE '*evaluate* educators are volunteers who have a heart for young people and a desire to change the sexual climate prevalent today. The *evaluate* programme enables educators to act as salt and light in schools.' The vision is to impact many thousands of young people by challenging attitudes and values, imparting knowledge and skills and empowering them to make healthy choices. CARE aims to make a real and lasting difference.[25]

CARE provides training for teams of educators who are accredited to deliver the *evaluate* programme and buy into the franchise, giving them the right to use the material and receive ongoing support.[26] CARE's prayer guide asks its supporters to continue to pray that God will bless their *evaluate* programme 'that complements the National Curriculum of Sex and Relationship Education'.[27] Sue Lindars would like to see teams promoting CARE's sex education programme in local churches, particularly as *evaluate* is an ideal way of bringing churches together. 'I'd like to see people going into churches to do recruitment events,' she said.[28]

Much of the information contained in this book is taken from CARE's *evaluate* website. Our purpose is to examine CARE's sex education programme with this question in mind. Is CARE's *evaluate* sex education project, which is being funded by the generous gifts of tens of thousands of Christians, consistent with the teachings of the Christian faith?

(Endnotes)

1 CARE's website, Vision, http://www.care.org.uk/Group/Group.aspx?id=10608
2 CARE's Prayer Guide, April to August 2007, 'Prayer, care and you're there!'
3 www.care.org.uk/Groups/30233/CARE/Campaigns/Equality
4 CARE, Reports & Financial Statements, IObbA43, For the year ended 31 March 2006
5 Website, Churches together in Britain and Ireland, Religion and belief consultative group, www.ctbi.org.uk/218/
6 *CARE Today*, Issue 17, Spring/Summer 2009, Celebrating the world's 'Magna Carta', p5
7 Ibid.
8 *Your school and sex education*, CARE, 1996, p3

9 *Sex and Relationship Education*, CARE for Education, 2001
10 ES Williams, *Lessons in Depravity*, Belmont House Publishing, 2003, pp281-282
11 *Parents First – Sex Education within the Home*, CARE, 1995, foreword
12 Ibid. p5
13 Ibid. p79
14 Ibid. p35
15 Teenage parenthood, A submission to the Social Exclusion Unit, CARE, November 1998, p5
16 Ibid. p7
17 Ibid. p9
18 Ibid. p9
19 Ibid. p10
20 CARE, Quite a Catch, CARE Centres Network, product code LO39
21 CARE, evaluate website, home page
22 Schools Prayer Network Website, evaluate - CARE's Education Initiative, Christian Values in SRE
23 *CARE Today*, Issue 10, Spring 2006, Sex in the Cities, p7
24 *CARE Today*, Issue 12, Winter 2006, p8
25 Schools Prayer Network Website, evaluate - CARE's Education Initiative
26 http://www.care.org.uk/Group/Group.aspx?id=17489
27 CARE's Prayer Guide, Making a Christian difference through prayer, April to August 2008, p20
28 *CARE Today*, Issue 17 Spring/Summer 2009, School teams go for growth

3

The sex education industry

What is going on in Christian sex education? To address this question we must understand something of the history and objectives of the sex education industry of which the Christian version has become a part. The development of CARE's sex education programme has not emerged from a deeper understanding of Scripture, but in response to a crisis in the sexual health of young people. CARE claims that there is a desperate need among young people for accurate and reliable information on sex and relationships, as we shall see in chapter 7. The *evaluate* programme has been developed to meet this need. In this chapter we also examine the link between sex education and the worldview of secular humanism.

The struggle over contraception

In the nineteenth century, the public discussion of contraception was considered to be offensive, indecent and against the moral mores of society. Everybody in British society, with the exception of a few radicals and 'new women', believed that sex outside of marriage was not only wrong, but shameful. Most people in society were aware of the biblical virtues of chastity, modesty and self-control, and so for an unmarried couple to live together in a sexual relationship was unthinkable and condemned in the strongest possible terms. But there was a small group of determined people who opposed the Christian gospel and longed for sexual liberation from what they regarded as the repressive morality of the Church.

Those at the forefront of the emerging sexual revolution, such as Annie Besant, Margaret Sanger and Marie Stopes, saw the promotion of contraception as an important weapon in the revolt against Christian moral standards. In 1908, in response to the growing attack on biblical standards in the area of sexual morality, the Bishops of the Anglican Community called upon 'all Christian people to discountenance the use of all artificial means of restriction as demoralizing to character and hostile to national welfare'. In other words, the Bishops were clearly stating that the use of artificial means of contraception was immoral.

Margaret Sanger – birth control propagandist

Margaret Sanger was the foremost propagandist for sexual liberation in twentieth century America. She devoted her life to the public promotion of contraception and saw sex education as the means for spreading her ideology to the wider world. In recognition of her lifelong work she was awarded the accolade of Humanist of the Year in 1957. Her vision of a worldwide birth control movement led to the creation of the International Planned Parenthood Federation (IPPF), an organisation that has always campaigned to make access to contraception, legal abortion and sex education accepted as human rights.[1]

In 1995, the IPPF and its 127 member family planning associations approved a Charter on Sexual and Reproductive Rights that was based on internationally recognised instruments of human rights. The IPPF policy on sex education recognizes 'the right of all young people to enjoy sex and express their sexuality in the way that they choose'. It upholds the right of young people to sex education that 'should enhance the independence and self-esteem of young people and provide them with the knowledge and confidence to make informed choices'.[2] The IPPF have been pioneers of comprehensive sex education in schools and have probably done more than any other organisation to promote premarital sex and abortion, and the distribution of condoms and emergency contraception.

Marie Stopes – founder of the FPA

When Margaret Sanger visited London in 1915 she met a young Marie Stopes who listened intently to her story of the struggle for birth control in the USA. Stopes felt inspired to start a similar campaign in Great Britain. It is probably true to say that the sex education movement in England started with the publication of Marie Stopes' book *Married Love* in 1918.

This sex manual sold over a million copies and made its author world famous as an expert in sexual matters. Yet such was the explicit nature of her writing that it shocked her publishers and academic colleagues who were still influenced by Victorian attitudes to sex and women.[3]

The editor of *John Bull* launched a powerful attack on the writings of Marie Stopes. 'Dr Stopes has unloaded on to the market a series of books – *Married Love, Wise Parenthood, Radiant Motherhood,* and the like – which contain the frankest and most intimate discussion of sexual matters that has ever been permitted in this country... The whole tendency of this raging, tearing propaganda... is profoundly mischievous. Its sole practical effect, as far as I am able to judge, is to impart a knowledge of "birth control" methods to people who ought to have no use of them... and while I cannot possibly gauge the feelings of this gifted author as she sees her scientific works paraded for sale in the company of pornographic French novels and other accessories of vice, I should be wanting in candour if I did not point out the plain moral implications of these things.'[4]

In a speech at the Criterion Theatre, Stopes claimed, 'I am out for a much greater thing than birth control. I am out to smash the tradition of organised Christianity, and to enthrone Christ's own tradition of wholesome, healthy, natural love towards sex life.'[5]

Marie Stopes founded the first birth control clinic in London in 1921 and by 1930 there were a dozen or so voluntary birth control clinics around the country. She proposed the motion to establish the National Birth Control Council, which changed its name to the Family Planning Association (FPA) in 1939. This organisation was to play a prominent role in developing the sex education industry in the UK.

Marie Stopes' contribution to the sexual revolution was to cultivate the myth of sexual ignorance and to legitimise the use of sexually explicit language. She propagated the idea that the public was ignorant about sex and this ignorance could only be overcome by explicit sexual information; as an expert propagandist she used every means of publicity to promote her ideas.

In the face of the propaganda onslaught of Marie Stopes, the Bishops of the sixth Lambeth Conference (1920) again warned against the use of unnatural means of contraception. There is no doubt that the Christian mind of the nineteenth and first part of the twentieth century believed that contraception was a moral evil and took a strong public stand on the issue. But those who sought liberation from what they saw as repressive Christian morality knew that the battle over contraception lay at the heart of their struggle. British society could only experience true sexual liberation when contraception was freely available to all, and without moral censure.

The campaign for liberation moved forward in leaps and bounds as the Christian Church became more liberal in its theology and lost its way in matters of sexual conduct. In 1930 the Anglican Bishops accepted, somewhat reluctantly, that there were certain circumstances in which contraception could be used 'provided this was done in the light of Christian principles'. By the late 1950s the thinking on contraception in the Church had moved so far that the Bishops no longer saw family planning as a moral evil but as a means for practising responsible parenthood. The Church had embraced the language of the International Planned Parenthood Federation.

A comprehensive contraceptive service

The gateway to sexual liberation opened wide when the FPA approved the use of oral contraception in the early 1960s. Separating sex and reproduction was thought to be an easy task and sex for pleasure was a tempting possibility. The FPA and Brook campaigned to make contraception available to unmarried single people, and even to children. The 1960s saw the opening of the first Brook clinic which specialised in providing contraception for children under the age of sexual consent. The seeds of sexual liberation that for years had been carefully cultivated by those who followed the godless philosophy of the sexual revolutionaries such as Sigmund Freud, Margaret Sanger, Marie Stopes and Alfred Kinsey, to mention some of the more important, could take root and bear its inevitable fruit. The revolt against biblical morality spread like a virus through society during the permissive decades of the 1960s and 70s, gaining momentum during the final decades of the twentieth century.

Traditional views of sexual conduct were rapidly forgotten as increasing numbers of young people, taking advantage of the opportunities offered by contraception, became sexually active. Predictably, the consequence was a rise in the numbers of sexual tragedies among young people. The answer, according to the permissive mindset of the time, was to make contraception more freely available to young people.

The FPA, which was growing in influence, supported by the British Medical Association, engaged in a vigorous campaign to persuade the Government to provide contraception to all, irrespective of age, free of charge on the National Health Service (NHS). The argument was that condoms, if they were readily available, would halt the alarming growth in the number of teenage abortions and reduce the growing incidence of STIs.

In a parliamentary debate in 1973 Lord Avebury, a distinguished supporter of the British Humanist Association, argued that the increasing number of abortions were evidence of the failure of contraceptive services in the UK.[6] He stated, in unequivocal terms, that the objective of a comprehensive contraceptive service was to reduce unwanted teenage pregnancies, abortions and STIs. Following the advice of Lord Avebury, and other like minded parliamentarians, in 1974, by an Act of Parliament, the British Government became responsible for supplying contraception to children under the age of sexual consent. And the most shocking aspect of the Act was that it permitted doctors to prescribe contraceptives to children without the knowledge or consent of their parents. The promoters of contraception promised that the rate of abortions, teenage pregnancies and STIs would be reduced by the free availability of contraception.

The FPA sets a target to reduce unwanted pregnancies

In 1976 the chairman of the FPA, Alastair Service, confidently announced targets to reduce the annual number of unwanted pregnancies and the annual number of abortions by half in the next 10 years. These targets would be met by improving sex education and by providing free contraceptives for children and young people.

The FPA and the Health Education Council were accepted as those with the special knowledge required to educate the nation's children about sex and contraception. In 1977 the Family Planning Information Service, funded by the Government, was set up to provide information to the public about the availability of free contraceptives. In its first two years the information service distributed 12 million leaflets to GPs, clinics, educational establishments and health promotion officers. The country was, without any doubt, being flooded with sex education material. The resource list prepared by the Health Education Council in 1977 was 23 pages long, including pamphlets and leaflets, posters and charts, films and filmstrips, slides, film loops and audiotapes, all providing information and resources for sex educators.

Over the next 10 years the FPA distributed over 50 million items of literature promoting contraception among young people. Yet by 1986 the FPA had conveniently forgotten its targets, and so had everybody else, and the reason is not difficult to see. In 1976 the number of abortions in England and Wales was 130 thousand—by 1986 it had increased to 172 thousand, a 32 per cent rise. Furthermore, illegitimate births among teenagers more than doubled, from 19.6 thousand in 1976 to 39.6 thousand a decade later. Clearly, the FPA's contraceptive campaign had not achieved its targets. The claim that contraceptive services for children would reduce teenage pregnancies was not supported by the evidence.

In 1987 the Government sent the leaflet *AIDS – Don't Die of Ignorance* to every household in the country with this message: 'Unless you are sure of your partner, always use a condom. This will reduce the risk of catching the virus.'

Health of the Nation target to reduce teenage conceptions

The *Health of the Nation* white paper, published in 1992, was the first attempt by government to provide a strategic approach to improving the health of the population. The strategy identified HIV/AIDS and sexual health as a priority area with a specific target to reduce the rate of conceptions among under-16s by at least 50 per cent by the year 2000. This meant reducing the rate from 9.5 to 4.8 per 1000 females aged 13-15.

The full weight of the NHS, working with local authorities and voluntary organisations, was directed towards achieving this target. All health authorities were required to produce sexual health strategies. Brook reported that the number of its branches that specialise in providing contraception to under-age children and are funded by health authorities had almost doubled. 'This expansion has been accompanied by a proliferation of other birth control services specifically designed for young people, as health authorities develop their strategies to meet the *Health of the Nation* targets.'[7]

The Health Education Authority's report, *Sexual Health* (1994), announced that sex education, which would persuade teenagers to practise 'safer sex' by using condoms, would play an important role in helping to reach this target. And this was particularly good news for the producers of condoms, who, in 1992, were already selling 150 million condoms per year, a 110 per cent increase since 1980. *Sexual Health* made the point that 'the condom market has a highly developed retail distribution network and one that has been expanded in recent years by the growth in the condom market and by efforts to make condoms more accessible to consumers'. Condoms were available from chemist shops, supermarkets, vending machines in pubs, family planning clinics, drugstores, garages, by mail order, and from convenience stores.

The Health Education Authority believed that 'a sexual culture which encourages teenagers to ask for and use contraception is as important as issues of access and quality of services'.[8] It saw itself engaged in a mission to change the sexual culture of the country, and it had the full backing of the Government and a vast amount of public money to achieve this end. Needless to say, the target to reduce teenage conceptions was not met. Indeed, despite the massive 'safer sex' campaign, the second half of the 1990s was characterised by an epidemic of sexually transmitted diseases among young people, and still no reduction in the teenage pregnancy or abortion rate—in 1998 the under-16 conception rate was 9.0 per 1000, virtually the same rate as when the target was set six years previously.

New Labour's target to reduce teenage conceptions

When New Labour came into power in 1997, that is 23 years after the British Government had made contraceptives freely available to children without their parents' knowledge or consent, it was clear that a comprehensive contraceptive service had failed to reduce teenage pregnancies. Undeterred, New Labour made the reduction of teenage conceptions a cornerstone of its health policy, asserting that the teenage conception rate had not declined because the campaign to promote contraception among children had not been robust enough. It was confident that making contraception even more readily available would reduce teenage conceptions. And so it set up a Teenage Pregnancy Unit to develop a strategy to reduce conceptions by 50% by 2010 from a baseline in 1998. This was to be accomplished by vigorous sex education and by making contraceptives easily available to schoolchildren, sometimes through school nurses and contraceptive clinics attached to schools. Prime Minister, Tony Blair, wrote in his foreword to the *Teenage Pregnancy* report, 'Every year some 90 thousand teenagers in England become pregnant. They include nearly 8 thousand who are under 16... As a country we can't afford to continue to ignore this shameful record.'[9]

The report concludes that 'the past three decades of sex education have amounted to *neglect*'. And worse, there has been a drift into the most serious error of all—moralising. Young people have not only been neglected, they have also been threatened by the moralisers. The Government's action plan is adamant: 'Preaching is rarely effective. Whether the Government likes it or not, young people decide what they're going to do about sex and contraception. Keeping them in the dark or preaching at them makes it *less* likely they'll make the right decision.'[10] The implication is clear—any attempt to introduce a moral dimension into the discussion on sex education and contraception is potentially harmful, for 'moralising', in the eyes of New Labour, makes children *less* likely to make the right decision.

The action plan included a national campaign that 'will target young people and parents with the facts about teenage pregnancy and parenthood, with advice on how to deal with the pressure to have sex, and with messages that underline the importance of using contraception if they do have sex'.[11] Local areas appointed teenage pregnancy coordinators whose task is to pull together the services that have a role in preventing teenage pregnancy. All local authorities and health authorities in England are jointly required to produce a strategy that outlines the actions they intend to take to meet the national target for reducing teenage conceptions. Progress towards the teenage conception target is a key performance indicator for Primary Care Trusts (PCTs).

Sex education guidance for schools (2000)

The Government's *Sex and Relationship Education Guidance*, issued to all schools and health authorities in England in July 2000, says that, 'Knowledge of the different types of contraception, and of access to, and availability of contraception is a major part of the Government's strategy to reduce teenage pregnancy.' [12] It follows that, 'Trained staff in secondary schools should be able to give young people full information about different types of contraception, including emergency contraception and their effectiveness.'[13] This means that children are to be given instruction in using contraception, and emergency contraception, and teachers can give children confidential advice about where to obtain contraception. According to the guidance, 'young people need to know not just what safer sex is and why it is important but also how to negotiate it with a partner'.[14]

The National Strategy for Sexual Health

The first ever *National Strategy for Sexual Health* was launched in 2001. 'This strategy's fundamental aim is to improve England's sexual health. We need to foster a culture of positive sexual health by making sure that everyone gets the information they need – without stigma, fear or embarrassment – so that they can take informed decisions to prevent STIs, including HIV…'[15] The strategy recognises that contraceptive services have a key role in protecting against both unplanned pregnancies and STIs. The Public Health white paper *Choosing Health* (November 2004) announced £40m for upgrading contraceptive services including an audit to identify and address gaps in the services.

In 2004 the Department of Health, which was growing desperate because of the slow progress toward its flagship target, again stressed the duty of health professionals to give children confidential advice on contraception. 'All services providing advice and treatment on contraception, sexual and reproductive health should produce an explicit confidentiality policy which reflects this guidance and makes it clear that young people under 16 have the same right to confidentiality as adults. Confidentiality policies should be prominently advertised, in partnership with health, education, youth and community services.'[16] This guidance

31

not only makes it a duty for health professionals to provide children with contraception, emergency contraception or even an abortion without the consent of their parents, but for these services to prominently advertise the fact to under-age children. In other words, children must be made aware that they can get their supply of contraceptives without the worry that their parents might find out.

By 2006 it was looking unlikely that the target would be met. Nevertheless in *Teenage Pregnancy Next Steps* (2006) the Government was doing its best to encourage those involved in the battle against teenage pregnancies: 'We have made significant improvements in making access to services easier for young people, who remain the group least likely to seek advice. In the recent Department of Health contraceptive service audit, 85% of PCTs report that they have commissioned new youth focused contraceptive services since the start of the Strategy and support is increasingly available in places where young people spend their time – in schools, Further Education colleges and other youth settings, often in partnership with the voluntary sector. This is particularly important for boys and young men, who are less likely to access advice and services in traditional settings... The national evaluation also shows more young people (especially boys) accessing school-based services.'[17]

Review of sex education

After three decades of intense sex education, in 2007 the Government announced a review because they believed that the delivery was still 'patchy'. A steering group was set up to look at how sex education in primary and secondary schools could be improved. The main recommendation of the review, which reported in October 2008, is that sex education should be a compulsory part of the national curriculum in primary and secondary schools under a new curriculum to be introduced in September 2010. However, because of opposition to this recommendation, a new review will look at the question of whether there should be an opt-out clause for parents who do not want their children to take part in the lessons.

The influence of secular humanism

The British Humanist Association has a deep commitment to comprehensive sex education and is a member of the Sex Education Forum. The Association has endorsed the Government's recommendation that sex education is made compulsory in primary and secondary schools in 2010.[18] The Humanist Association 'believes that all children are entitled to full and accurate SRE (sex and relationships education) including unbiased information on contraception, STDs, abortion, sexual orientation, and the many forms of family relationship conducive to individual fulfilment and the stability of society... We believe that SRE can best be improved if it is a statutory, compulsory part of the curriculum in all schools, being comprehensive in scope and well above the minimum basics of what is currently required by law... The focus of SRE should be to equip children and young people with the capacity to make informed responsible choices about their own behaviour and activity.'

The Association asserts that 'in terms of private sexual behaviour, ethics and morals should be discussed in an open and objective way. No relationship should be condemned or taught as sinful or unnatural – the focus should be on maximising choice, personal responsibility and happiness, and against hurt, exploitation and coercion. Good SRE would teach about the importance of the family, recognising that increasingly in today's society, the family can take many forms, and that same sex civil partnerships are now recognised in law alongside heterosexual marriage.'[19]

Uptake of contraception by children

Here we should note that the campaign of successive Governments to increase the use of contraception among children has been remarkably successful. The trend in contraceptive use among girls under 16 years of age (that is, under the age of sexual consent) shows a massive, tenfold increase over the last two and a half decades. In 1975, around 8 thousand under-16s visited to a community contraceptive clinic and by 2006 the figure had risen to 83 thousand (figure page 34). The effect of this increase meant that in 2006 around 5% of girls aged 13-14, and 15% of girls aged 15, were visiting a community clinic for their supply of contraceptives.[20] The peak age for attendance, however, was among girls aged 16 and 17,

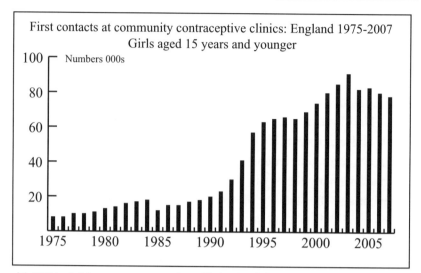

First contacts at community contraceptive clinics: England 1975-2007
Girls aged 15 years and younger

with 22% visiting a contraception clinic. And these figures do not include services provided by consultants in out-patient clinics or those provided by general practitioners.

Despite these alarming statistics, the Government is doing all in its power to increase still further the use of contraceptives among under-age children. The latest outrage is a plan to introduce a national condom card scheme for 13-year-old boys. How many more children under the age of sexual consent does the Government want to be using contraceptives?

Yet progress towards the Government's conception target has been surprisingly slow, and by 2007 it was obvious that the target would not be met. Latest figures suggest a reduction of around 11% from the 1998 baseline. But if a more robust baseline had been chosen, namely a three year average from 1994 to 1996, then the reduction in teenage concep-tions is a miserly 3%. In other words, the Government's contraception campaign has been a complete failure for it has not significantly reduced the teenage conception rate. Indeed the under-18 conception rate in 2007 of 41.9 per 1000 females aged 15-17 is the same as the rate in 1994 and 1995 (figure page 35).[21]

The fruit of the sexual revolution

By the beginning of the twenty-first century, after three decades of intense sex education, the traditional restraints on sexual behaviour have

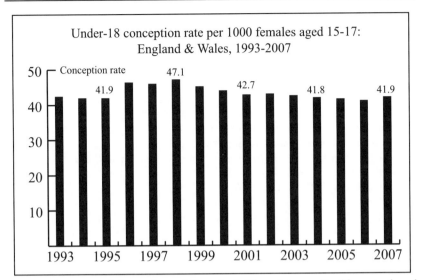

Under-18 conception rate per 1000 females aged 15-17:
England & Wales, 1993-2007

been all but erased from the public mind. The virtues of self-control and modesty are seen as irrelevant ideas that have no place in a sexually liberated society. Marriage has become devalued and cohabitation is the norm among young couples. Just under half of the babies born in the UK are now born outside of wedlock. Promiscuity is widespread and children are becoming sexually active at increasingly younger ages. Indeed, in today's society it is accepted as the norm for teenagers to be sexually active and tens of thousands of children under the age of sexual consent are visiting family planning clinics for their supply of contraceptives.

Yet sexual freedom has its inevitable consequences, as many young people are finding out to their cost. So grave is the problem of unintended teenage pregnancy that children are being injected with long-acting contraceptives without their parents' knowledge or consent. The latest desperate initiative is for contraception and emergency contraception to be advertised on radio and TV at any time during the day or night. Sexually transmitted diseases are so rampant that there is a chlamydia screening programme for young people. Emergency contraception is being widely used by young women and abortion rates continue at unacceptable levels. The sexual revolution has done its terrible work—sexual immorality is rife and young lives are being ruined.

(Endnotes)

1 The Human Right to Family Planning, International Planned Parenthood Federation, 1984, p6

2 IPPF Framework for Comprehensive Sexuality Education, produced by the IPPF Adolescents Team, London, May 2006, page 2

3 June Rose, *Marie Stopes and the Sexual Revolution*, Faber and Faber, London, 1992, p100

4 John Bull, 8 April 1922, cited from *Marie Stopes and the Sexual Revolution*, p157

5 *Daily Mirror*, 16 March 1925, cited from Ruth Hall, *Marie Stopes*, p260

6 Hansard, Lords debate, 12 February 1973, c1338

7 Brook Advisory Centres, Annual Report, 1992/93, p1

8 Health Education Authority, *Health Update, 4 Sexual Health*, Joanna Goodrich, Henrietta Lang and Mary Sayers, 1994, p26

9 *Teenage pregnancy*, HMSO, London, June 1999, p4

10 Ibid. p90

11 Ibid. p8

12 *Sex and Relationship Education Guidance*, DfEE, July 2000, p15

13 Ibid. p15

14 Ibid. p18

15 *National Sexual health and HIV strategy*, Department of Health, December 2001, p12

16 Department of Health, Gateway reference number, 3382, 29 July 2004, Best practice guidance for doctors and other health professionals on the provision of advice and treatment to young people under 16 on contraception, sexual and reproductive health

17 *Teenage Pregnancy Next Steps: Guidance for Local Authorities and Primary Care Trusts on Effective Delivery of Local Strategies*, Department for Education and Skills, July 2006, p42

18 Sex and Relationships Education Review 2008. Note for the Sex Education Forum from the British Humanist Association.

19 British Humanist Association, 'delighted' that SRE to become compulsory in all schools, 23 October 2008

20 NHS Contraceptive Services, England, 2006-07, The Information Centre, National Statistics, Table 2, First contacts at community contraceptive clinics by gender and age 1996-97 to 2006-07

21 Office for National Statistics, Conception statistics 2007 (provisional)

4

God's plan for sexual conduct and

the sexual revolution

To form a true judgement of CARE's sex education programme, and to know what Christian parents should teach their children, we need to understand what Scripture teaches about sexual conduct. God's plan for sexual conduct and marriage is one of the most profound teachings of the Bible, for it forms the basis of family life and is the foundation on which a stable society is built. It has been believed and accepted by most people in Great Britain for the last thousand years and brought great blessing to our nation. Because God's plan for sexual conduct is based in divine wisdom it has a great appeal to the human heart. Those who hear God's plan know in their conscience that what they are hearing is divine truth.

The sexual nature of mankind

Scripture makes it clear that sex is God's idea. The God of the Bible, who created human beings in his own image, created mankind male and female. In his great wisdom God created human beings who would reproduce sexually. He could have chosen a non-sexual way of repro- duction, but he did not do so. God had sex in mind right from the very beginning of creation. After God had created the first man (Adam) and woman (Eve), he saw that his creation, including our sexual nature, was very good. So our sexual nature is part of God's perfect creation, one of God's greatest gifts to mankind.

God's first command to mankind was to be fruitful and multiply (Genesis 1:28). As we shall see, it is God's will that children should be born into the family created at the time of marriage. God created the first man (Adam) from the dust of the earth. And the LORD God said, 'It is not good that man should be alone; I will make him a helper comparable to him' (Genesis 2:18). God caused the man to fall into a deep sleep, and created the first woman (Eve) from a rib taken from the side of the man. This is an important truth, for it shows the closeness of the relationship between the sexes.

The marriage ordinance

The first marriage is described in the second chapter of Genesis. God brings the woman to Adam and he cries out with delight, 'This is now bone of my bones, and flesh of my flesh: she shall be called Woman, because she was taken out of Man' (Genesis 2:23). God ordained marriage with these words: 'Therefore a man shall leave his father and mother and be joined to his wife, and they shall become one flesh' (Genesis 2:24). The symbolism of the rib provides a picture of marriage, for at marriage the rib returns into the man, as husband and wife become one flesh; they are no longer two separate individuals but one entity—a new family. There is something so deep and wonderful in the marriage bond that we need spiritual insight to understand its divine significance. Scripture uses the unity between Christ and his Church as a symbol of the marriage union of husband and wife.

Jesus emphasized the one flesh union created at marriage with the words: 'So then, they are no longer two but one flesh. Therefore what God has joined together, let not man separate' (Matthew 19:6). The one flesh union is complete when the couple consummate their marriage union by sexual intercourse. Husband and wife lovingly share their sexual life, accepting that their union is likely to be blessed by the birth of children. They accept with joy the children that result, for they are the natural, legitimate products of their marriage—clear evidence that they are truly one flesh. The concept of one flesh is illustrated by the children who are born into the family. Both parents contribute equally to the genetic make up of their children, and the likeness to their parents witnesses to this fact. Biblical teaching makes it clear that a family is formed by the marriage of a man and a woman. Without marriage, there is no family.

According to Jesus, it is God who joins a husband and wife in marriage. And so we see a profound biblical truth— families are created by God, and not by man. Those who marry must understand that they have entered into a lifelong union; there is no turning back, no second chance, for the marriage vow is 'till death us do part'. This is why it is so important for husband and wife to remain faithful to each other.

The maternal instinct

Because womankind is created in the image of God, women have an inborn understanding of the maternal role. The first woman was named Eve, 'because she was the mother of all living' (Genesis 3:20). God has created women in such a way that it is natural for most to desire marriage and motherhood. Most women understand that children should be born into a family created by marriage. God has placed within the conscience of womankind a natural inhibition to restrain them from abusing the gift of motherhood. Their conscience warns that sex outside marriage is wrong, and they fear the consequences of an unintended pregnancy.

The biblical virtues

In his great wisdom God has instituted moral laws around human sexual conduct that are expressed in the four virtues—modesty, self-control, chastity and fidelity. While each virtue applies to an aspect of sexual behaviour, together they form a coherent inner belief system that expresses the biblical attitude to sex, marriage and the family. Sexual purity is the foundation on which these virtues are built. Marriage flourishes when all four virtues are practised. 'Marriage is honourable in all, and the bed undefiled; but fornicators and adulterers God will judge' (Hebrews 13:4). And most important of all, these are the God-given virtues that protect children from the ravages that result from sexual immorality.

The virtue of chastity

The concept of chastity flows from the holiness that is central to the character of God. Because God is holy, he demands sexual purity among his people. 'It is God's will that you should be holy; that you should avoid sexual immorality; that each of you should learn to control his own body in a way that is holy and honourable, not in passionate lust like the heathen, who do not know God... For God did not call us to be impure, but to live a holy life' (1 Thessalonians 4:3-8 NIV). Young women are to be trained 'to be discreet, chaste' (Titus 2:5). The word chaste, which is related to the word holy, means clean, modest, pure, undefiled. As the word 'holy' means to be separated from sin, so the word 'chaste' means to be separated from sexual impurity. The above verses make it clear that those who seek to follow the way of Christ should learn to control their passions and desires in a way that is honourable and pure.

The standard that God has set for his people is that we should be pure in body and spirit. Jesus said, 'Blessed are the pure in heart, for they shall see God' (Matthew 5:8). The message of the apostle Paul is 'keep yourself pure' (1 Timothy 5:22), and he instructs Timothy to relate to young women 'with all purity' (1 Timothy 5:2). Sexual purity, or chastity, is an attitude of the heart and mind that comes from an understanding of God's holy character and is manifest in the way we think, the way we talk and the way we behave.

One of the essential marks of Christian conduct is purity of speech. Christian believers are to rid themselves of 'filthy language' (Colossians 3:8). They should let no corrupt word proceed out of their mouths (Ephesians 4:29) and there must not be 'filthiness, nor foolish talking, nor coarse jesting, which are not fitting' (Ephesians 5:4). The Bible warns that no immoral or impure person 'has any inheritance in the kingdom of Christ and of God' (Ephesians 5:5). We can be sure that Christian people do not indulge in lewd and indecent language. The sex talk promoted by sex educators is unacceptable to God's holy people.

Jesus condemns the lustful look as equivalent to adultery and the apostle John warns that 'the lust of the flesh, the lust of the eyes, and the pride of life—is not of the Father but is of the world (1 John 2:16). Indeed, the lust of the eyes is so dangerous that Jesus says, 'If your right eye causes you to sin, pluck it out and cast it from you' (Matthew 5:29). So Christians are warned of the moral danger of tolerating sexual impurity. The sexual images of the sex educators are anathema to the Christian faith.

An attitude of mind that seeks after sexual purity is at the heart of biblical teaching. Implicit within the idea of purity is an undivided heart which renounces sensual and sexual pollution, and a spirit of obedience to God's moral law. A pure heart inculcates a duty of self-restraint and self-denial. The people of God desire purity in all areas of their lives, and especially in sexual relationships.

Sexual abstinence

Here we must emphasise that the concept of sexual abstinence is *not* a biblical virtue. Advising young people to delay the onset of sexual intercourse until they are in a committed relationship, is the message of sex education not the Bible. All sex education programmes advise those who feel they are not yet ready to say: 'No, I don't want to have sex with you now.' Some people are misled into believing that this message, which encourages young people to delay the onset of sexual intercourse, is consistent with biblical morality. But this is not the case. Delaying the onset of sexual intercourse, or abstinence, or learning to wait until the right moment, is a pragmatic decision based on the feelings and desires of the young people involved, and has nothing to do with what is right or wrong. Chastity is completely different—it's a choice based on obedience to God's moral law, motivated by a desire to do what is right in God's eyes and a desire for sexual purity. There is a world of difference between the pragmatic, amoral advice offered by abstinence education and the Bible's teaching on chastity.

As we have seen, the ABC approach to sex education, which some people claim is consistent with biblical teaching, offers a pragmatic choice between abstaining from sex (or delaying sex until in a committed relationship) or using a condom. It is important to remember the compromise behind the abstinence message.

The virtue of modesty

Modesty is the virtue that recognises the rightful purpose of sex as something that is private, mysterious, and meant for the relationship between husband and wife. Modesty reveals the inner beauty and moral strength of a woman, for her beauty does not come from her outward appearance but from 'the hidden person of the heart, with the incorruptible beauty of a gentle and quiet spirit, which is very precious in the sight of God' (1 Peter 3:4). The apostle Paul emphasises the importance of women adorning 'themselves in modest apparel, with propriety and moderation, not with braided hair or gold or pearls or costly clothing' (1 Timothy 2:9). Modesty teaches a woman to cover herself in a way that is discreet and decent, and reveals itself in the way a woman dresses, talks and behaves. A modest woman does not make a show of her sexual attributes. She hides her eyes from explicit images, closes her ears to explicit talk and guards her mind from impure thoughts. The immodest woman is destroying her woman-hood by her foolish behaviour.

So the true beauty of a woman comes from her moral character. The great value of modesty is that it enhances the feminine attributes of womankind. It produces a woman of resolute character who understands the value of her sexuality. Her relationships with men are based on truth and genuine affection, not on sexual lust. She is not a sex object, but a woman with dignity and value. She is not sexually provocative, for she understands the value of chastity and why sexual intercourse should be reserved for marriage. By her modest behaviour she earns the respect of men, and they desire her companionship because of who she is, not because she is sexually available. And more, modesty makes a woman attractive to the one man who chooses her to be his wife.

The message of sex education, which aims to uncover sex by using explicit words and images, is the antithesis of modest behaviour. The false teaching of 'safer sex' encourages a woman to make herself appear to be sexual available.

The virtue of self-control

Scripture exhorts young men to be self-controlled and to deny ungodliness and worldly lusts (Titus 2:12). Like modesty, self-control is a virtue that reveals the inner moral strength of a man. It is a mindset that strives to live according to God's word, to have a pure mind and clean hands. It is a way of life that compels a man to treat women with honour and respect, recognising that they are the weaker partner in that they are sexually vulnerable through pregnancy, childbirth and motherhood (1 Peter 3:7).

A self-controlled, honourable man is courteous and caring towards women, and does not take sexual advantage. He is not ruled by sexual lust, does not treat women as sex objects and rejects casual sex as wrong.

A young man who wants to keep himself pure must flee the lusts and passions of the flesh and pursue righteousness out of a pure heart (2 Timothy 2:22). Jesus said that whoever looks at a woman with lust in his eyes has already committed adultery with her in his heart (Matthew 5:28). A self-controlled young man will avoid any situation in which he is likely to face sexual temptation and will keep away from the immoral woman. 'Do not lust after her beauty in your heart, nor let her allure you with her eyelids. For by means of a harlot a man is reduced to a crust of bread; and an adulteress will prey upon his precious life. Can a man take fire to his bosom, and his clothes not be burned?' (Proverbs 6:25-27).

Children and young people who have been taught the biblical virtues of chastity, modesty and self-control, gain no benefit from being told about contraceptive techniques and how to 'be prepared' for sex. Those who have been taught the biblical standard of sexual purity will regard the explicit images of sex education as pornographic, and will object to the use of lewd language. Having learned the biblical principles of sexual conduct, they do not need to be taught the facts about condoms or the details of STIs that sex educators take a sordid pleasure in teaching.

The lusts of the flesh

Having seen the wonder of God's plan for sexual conduct we need to recognise that all mankind struggles against the lusts of the flesh which war against the soul (1 Peter 2:11). 'We all once conducted ourselves in the lusts of our flesh, fulfilling the desires of the flesh and of the mind, and were by nature children of wrath' (Ephesians 2:3). Because all people are sinners by nature, all people are subject to sexual temptation. This means that relationships between the sexes are fraught with difficulties. Because of the lusts of the flesh young men and women should do all they can to avoid sexual temptation. Young men are especially tempted into lustful thoughts by images of the female body. 'But each one is tempted when he is drawn away by his own desires and enticed. Then, when desire has conceived, it gives birth to sin; and sin, when it is full-grown, brings forth death' (James 1:14-15). One of the reasons why sex education is so wrong is because it encourages impure thoughts, inflames lustful desires and leads to sexual temptation.

But Christian young people, with the help of the Holy Spirit, can know victory over sexual temptation and can lead a pure life for God has promised, 'No temptation has overtaken you except such as is common to man; but God is faithful, who will not allow you to be tempted beyond what you are able, but with the temptation will also make the way of escape, that you may be able to bear it' (1 Corinthians 10:13).

The Bible gives the strongest possible warning against sexual immorality. The message is insistent—flee sexual immorality (1 Corinthians 6:18). All immorality and impurity and uncontrolled passion are to be put to death for these things, which belong to the sons of disobedience, bring the wrath of God (Colossians 3:5-6). 'But fornication and all uncleanness or covetousness, let it not even be named among you, as is fitting for saints' (Ephesians 5:3). Scripture is clear; sexual immorality, impurity and uncontrolled passion must not even be hinted at, much less practised, by God's people.

The reason sexual sin is so terrible in God's eyes is because 'he who commits sexual immorality sins against his own body. Or do you not know that your body is the temple of the Holy Spirit who is in you, whom you have from God, and you are not your own? For you were bought at a price; therefore glorify God in your body and in your spirit, which are God's' (1 Corinthians 6:18-20). Scripture teaches that our souls as well as our bodies belong to God. Our body is the temple of the Holy Spirit, therefore to sin sexually is to defile the temple of God. And we know that this is true, for all around are the dreadful consequences of sexual sin.

The message of 'safer sex' is destructive because it condones sexual immorality, and those who fall into this sin are harming their own body. Even those who manage to avoid an unintended pregnancy or STI, still have the problem of a bad conscience, for they know in their heart that sex outside marriage is not only foolish, but also wrong. The momentary pleasure of illicit sex is not worth the heavy cost demanded by sexual immorality.

We have seen that only the Bible, God's Word, provides a sure, trustworthy guide to sexual conduct. The teaching of Scripture is the rule for life and sexual conduct; therefore, the message of 'safer sex' has no place in Christian thinking or practice.

Parents should teach their children God's moral law

Scripture instructs parents to teach their children the moral law of God, for his laws are righteous and good. 'And these words which I command you today shall be in your heart. You shall teach them diligently to your children, and shall talk of them when you sit in your house, when you walk by the way, when you lie down, and when you rise up... And teach them to your children and your grandchildren' (Deuteronomy 6: 6-7, 4:9). The home environment is the place where children are brought up in the training and instruction of the Lord. Parents should teach their children God's plan for sexual conduct.

Here we should remind ourselves that Scripture does not use the word sex. Every reference to sexual activity in the Bible is made in euphemistic terms. In biblical times it was the Canaanites who were obsessed with sex and used children in sexual rituals. The people of God, on the other hand, talked to their children about the law of God and the moral standards by which they ought to live. The assertion of CARE that parents should talk to their children about sex is contrary to biblical teaching. Exposing children to sex talk is unnatural, an assault on the innocence of childhood and a subtle form of child abuse. Moreover, because of the moral imperative that surrounds sexual behaviour, because children know in their conscience that certain forms of behaviour are wrong, they can only be confused and embarrassed by the crass attempts of their parents to talk about sex. Indeed, most children are deeply embarrassed by the thought of discussing the details of sex, condoms and STIs with their mother or father. It is wrong for parents to engage in explicit sex talk with their children.

When it comes to sexual behaviour, a wise parent recognises that God has given children a time of innocence during which they should be taught the difference between right and wrong. Slowly, as they mature, children learn to understand the mystery of their sexual nature. They absorb the differences between male and female by living with their parents and siblings in a family. As they observe the different roles of their father and mother in everyday family life, they slowly discern the differences in behaviour and dress, and the way their father and mother relate to each other. They see that their father and mother love each other, share a bed together, and sleep together. The family situation with parents, brothers and sisters feels secure, natural and right and gives a great sense of belonging.

As children slowly mature into adolescence they have the model of their parents and family as an example. They hear the way the members of the family speak to each other and soon realise that explicit, foul, obscene language has no place in the family situation. And children that grow up in a home where their father and mother love and respect each other, see a model of what marriage and family relationships should be and come to understand the importance of faithfulness in a sexual relationship.

Because sexuality is a part of human nature, as children grow older and pass through puberty it is natural for them gradually to understand how their body functions. (Adam and Eve did not need sex education). As children become aware of their sexual nature, they should do so in accordance with the moral standards that they have learned from their parents. They develop moral beliefs about sexual conduct in the context of their parents' marriage, the standards implicit within their family, and from the message of the Bible. As they grow into adolescence they do not need to be taught about sexual techniques and condoms, for they have already learnt that certain forms of behaviour, such as sexual promiscuity, are plainly wrong. They also know that such behaviour is not only wrong but would cause deep distress to their parents and family.

It is natural for a mother to prepare her daughter for womanhood and menstruation. It is also natural for parents to answer the questions that their children ask about sex in an honest and thoughtful way, taking account of the child's age. But just as parents do not need to teach children how to walk or talk, for they learn these skills naturally as they grow older, so they do not need to teach children the details of sexual physiology, for children come to understand their sexual nature as they mature into adulthood. Daughters learn from their mothers to dress and behave with modesty, and not to encourage sexual advances from boys. Sons learn to respect their mother and to behave with decency and honour towards women. They are taught to treat all women as they treat their mother, and most young men are very protective of their mother's honour. A well brought up young man knows that he should not take advantage of a young woman.

There is, of course, the issue of those children who grow up in single parent homes, who do not have the model of a family as a guide for their behaviour. One reason children from single parent homes are especially prone to sexual tragedies, is that they do not have the same degree of moral teaching that is implicit in the family situation. It is especially important, therefore, that children who grow up in such situations should be taught the moral framework of the Bible. Those who claim that such children are offended by being taught about the importance of marriage and the family are wrong. Children from broken homes (like the author) and single parent homes know of the joys of a proper family, and desperately want something better for themselves. It is completely wrong to withhold the Christian teaching of marriage on the pretext of upsetting children whose parents are not married.

Sexual immorality among God's people

Sexual immorality is hateful to God because it destroys marriage, the family and the nation. Scripture reports the events of Numbers 25 in careful detail to serve as a warning of the dreadful consequences of sexual immorality among God's people. It also serves as a warning to those who seek to introduce sexual immorality into the Church.

The King of Moab, Balak, sought the prophet Balaam the son of Beor to curse the people of Israel. When he was prevented by God from cursing Israel, the mad prophet, who loved the wages of wickedness, devised a wicked plan to lead Israel into sexual immorality with the women of Moab.

While in Shittim, the Israelite men began to whore with the daughters of Moab, yoking themselves to the Baal of Peor and sacrificing to the gods of the Moabites. Scripture informs us that the prophet Balaam was behind this terrible rebellion. Such was the mad prophet's love for money that he devised a subtle plan—he taught Balak to encourage Moabite women to entice the men of Israel into sexual immorality. Balaam knew the power of sexual immorality to destroy the people of God, for he understood the link between sexual immorality and idolatry.

The sexual immorality of Israel was so blatant that one man, Zimri, brought his Midianite lover, Cozbi, into his family tent in the sight of

47

Moses and the whole congregation. In open contempt for God's law, Zimri engaged in sexual sin with the woman. Phinehas, the son of Eleazar the priest, understood the terrible sin that was being committed, and in his zeal for God's honour took a spear and thrust it through the man and the woman, evidently engaged in a sexual act.

God's judgement on the offenders was swift, severe and public. The Lord said to Moses, 'Take all the leaders of the people and hang the offenders before the Lord, out in the sun, that the fierce anger of the Lord may turn away from Israel.' The Lord decreed the execution of the leaders for they bore responsibility for what had happened. So Moses said to the judges of Israel, 'Every one of you kill his men who were joined to Baal of Peor' (Numbers 25:4-5).

The Lord commanded the community to bring the offenders to be judged, to show they would not accept this kind of sin in their midst. Phinehas in his righteous zeal understood the shocking nature of the sin of Israel, and that the Lord would not tolerate sexual immorality among his people. Sexual immorality had to be judged and dealt with severely. And to underline the appalling nature of sexual immorality among God's people, the Lord caused 24 thousand Israelites to die by the plague.

God commanded his prophet Moses to take vengeance on those who enticed Israel into sexual sin. 'Arm some of yourselves for war, and let them go against the Midianites to take vengeance for the Lord on Midian' (Numbers 31:3). The Israelites killed all the men and the kings of Midian. They also killed Balaam son of Beor with the sword. And Moses said to them: 'Have you kept all the women alive? Look, these women caused the children of Israel, through the counsel of Balaam, to trespass against the Lord in the incident of Peor, and there was a plague among the congregation of the Lord. Now therefore, kill every male among the little ones, and kill every woman who has known a man intimately' (Numbers 31:16-17). The warning of Scripture is clear—those who introduce sexual immorality among God's people face the fury of God's vengeance.

The apostle Peter, warning of false prophets, mentions the example of Balaam, who loved the wages of unrighteousness (2 Peter 2:15-16). Our Lord makes the connection between Balaam's unsuccessful attempt to curse Israel and the subsequent idolatry: 'But I have a few things against you, because you have there those who hold the doctrine of Balaam, who taught Balak to put a stumbling block before the children of Israel, to eat things sacrificed to idols, and to commit sexual immorality' (Revelation 2:14).

Rebellion against God's plan for sexual conduct

We live in a fallen world in which there is a spiritual war between good and evil. 'For we do not wrestle against flesh and blood, but against principalities, against powers, against the rulers of the darkness of this age, against spiritual hosts of wickedness in the heavenly places' (Ephesians 6:12). The rulers of darkness, following in the footsteps of Balaam, are engaged in a concerted attack on the divine plan for sexual conduct. The sexual revolutionaries, people such as Margaret Sanger, Marie Stopes and Wilhelm Reich (a disciple of Freud) have devoted their lives to the struggle for sexual liberation—they want freedom to engage in sexual activity without moral restraint or judgement.

The Sexual Revolution, written by Wilhelm Reich, is an important book for it provides a clear statement of the objectives of the sexual revolution. Reich made it clear that the aim is to allow people to enjoy sexual gratification without moral restraint. He believed that Christian morality was the underlying cause of sexual repression, concluding that the institution of lifelong marriage, which is grounded in traditional morality, acts as a brake on sexual reform. So the great enemy, in the mind of the sexual revolutionaries, is traditional marriage for it upholds and strengthens moral standards in society.

Reich saw that sex education was an important vehicle for propagating the ideas of the sexual revolution among children. He believed that the promotion of nakedness was a crucial part of sex education. Reich asserted that 'with our approval of nakedness, with our sexual education... we are pulling one stone after the other from the edifice of conservative morality; that the ideal of virginity until marriage becomes as hollow as that of eternal monogamy, and with that the ideal of conventional marriage in general. For no sensible person will contend that people who have had a sex education which is serious, uncompromising and based on science, will be able to conform to the prevailing compulsive customs and morality.'[1]

Reich was adamant that the sexual revolution could only succeed once the biblical virtues of modesty and self-control had first been wiped from the public mind. He saw marriage and the family as the bastions of traditional morality that needed to be undermined for the revolution to succeed.

A theme that runs through *Lessons in Depravity* is that the aim of the sexual revolution is to purge biblical morality from the minds of children and young people. After carefully documenting the association between the sexual revolution and sex education, I concluded:

> We can only understand the motivation behind sex education if we grasp
> the essential point that it has evolved out of the ideas of the sexual revolu-
> tion... In my opinion, the real objective of sex education is, and always
> has been, to promote the amoral ideology of the sexual revolution. In
> this, it has been remarkably successful.[2]

The war of the two seeds

The sexual revolution can only be fully understood when it is placed in a biblical context. The third chapter of Genesis describes the fall of man and its consequences. When Adam and Eve rebelled against God's command and ate the forbidden fruit, their eyes were opened and they knew that they were naked. So they sewed together fig leaves for coverings and when they heard God walking in the Garden they hid themselves from his presence. When God asked Adam if he had eaten of the forbidden fruit, Adam blamed the woman for giving him the fruit of the tree, and the woman blamed the serpent, 'The serpent deceived me, and I ate' (Genesis 3:13). So God cursed the serpent, Satan, who had deceived the woman and said, 'And I will put enmity between you and the woman, and between your seed and her Seed; He shall bruise your head, and you shall bruise His heel' (Genesis 3:15).

Here we learn from Scripture of the battle between the seed of Satan, described by our Lord as children of the devil (John 8:44), and the Seed of the woman, who is Christ and his Church. The apostle Paul refers to the prince of the power of the air (Satan), 'the spirit who now works in the sons of disobedience' (Ephesians 2:2). According to Matthew Henry, 'A perpetual quarrel is here commenced between the kingdom of God and the kingdom of the devil among men; war is proclaimed between the

Seed of the woman and the seed of the serpent.' This is a spiritual war against the rulers of the darkness of this age, against spiritual hosts of wickedness in high places referred to in Ephesians 6.

Today the war between the seed of the serpent and the Seed of the woman has reached a new intensity. The seed of the serpent is manifest in the godless ideology of secular humanism, an ideology that is at total war with the Christian Church.

Secular humanism is a worldview that rejects the God of Scripture and his moral law. Over recent decades it has become the dominant ideology in the UK and is represented by the British Humanist Association, the National Secular Society and many leading opinion formers, media personalities and academics. It seeks to create a society that is ruled by rational thought alone, without recourse to the God of Scripture. It rejects the idea of an absolute moral law, and wants a society where every person is free to do what is right in their own eyes.

At the heart of secular humanism is a deep hostility to God's plan for marriage and the family, and the biblical virtues that protect marriage. Secular humanism has played a prominent role in the development of sex education, which it sees as a vehicle for inculcating its godless ideas into the minds of children. Just as Satan deceived Eve in the Garden of Eden, casting doubt on the truth of God's word, so today he deceives mankind by challenging God's plan for sexual conduct and marriage as being no longer relevant in a modern sexually liberated world.

The sexual revolution is an important front in the spiritual war between the seed of the serpent and the Seed of the woman. To understand the motivation that drives the sex education industry, we must recognise and understand the spiritual war that is being waged against the divine plan for sexual conduct. Having established the links between the sex education industry, the sexual revolution and the worldview of secular humanism, we are now in a position to examine CARE's sex education policy.

(Endnotes)

1 Wilhelm Reich, *The Sexual Revolution*, translated by Theodore Wolfe, Vision Press, 1969, p66
2 ES Williams, *Lessons in Depravity*, Belmont House Publishing, 2003, p241

5

CARE's sex education policy

Following decades of intensive sex education there is a crisis in the sexual health of young people. Professor Michael Adler, a key Government adviser, warns that sexual health clinics are struggling to cope with demand. He said: 'It is no exaggeration that we now face a public health crisis in relation to sexual health. Sexual health is not an NHS or political priority. Until it becomes so, we will witness further failure upon further failure.'[1] But why does he say that sexual health is not a political priority when, as we saw in chapter 3, it has received massive political attention and funding? Is this another excuse for the failure of sex education? And the failure has not been in persuading young people to use contraception. Indeed, the promotion of contraception has been very successful; the failure has been that contraception has not delivered the promised benefits. The claims of the condom promoters have proved to be an illusion.

The large number of children who are being recruited into contraception each year is indicative of widespread sexual immorality that must be disturbing to the Christian mind. The idea that the State provides children of any age, yes any age, even 10 and 11-year-olds, with contraception behind their parents' back is morally indefensible.

In the face of this crisis there is great political and religious confusion. What should be done? Nobody, it seems, is sure how to deal with the crisis. The Church is strangely silent, and most Christians are reluctant to become involved. The incessant cry of the secular humanist lobby, led by the Government's Teenage Pregnancy Unit, and spurred on by the FPA, Brook and the Sex Education Forum, is for more sex education starting at an even younger age, easier access to contraception and more emergency contraception. The Institute for Public Policy Research has recently recommended that children of 10 should be taught about contraception in their final year at primary school, and Brook is working with the Government to develop a national condom card scheme for 13-year-old boys. Yet the special pleading of the sex education lobby is beginning to wear a bit thin, for it must be obvious to any objective observer that more contraception is not the answer.

CARE's response to the crisis, as we saw in chapter 2, has been to develop a new programme, *evaluate... informing choice* that aims to bring a fresh edge to sex education. The *evaluate* webpage for teachers explains: 'Young people today are confronted with many challenges and pressures and need a secure and safe environment in which to examine what they know, *develop their own values* [my italics] and acquire the life skills necessary to make and carry out healthy decisions.'[2]

The aims of CARE's sex education policy

The aims of CARE's policy have been downloaded from the *evaluate* website. I have added italics to draw attention to important principles.

The aims of *evaluate... informing choice* are to:

- provide education which is interactive, developmental in its approach and is both cognitively challenging and appropriate

- empower, equip and enable young people *to make healthy informed choices*

- encourage young people to see themselves as valuable and unique individuals, thus motivating them to make wise and healthy choices particularly in relation to their sexual and drug taking behaviour

- support young people in *delaying sexual experience until a committed relationship*, ideally marriage

- see the high rates of teenage pregnancy and Sexually Transmitted Infections in the UK reduced

- be a voice into society affirming marriage and faithfulness in relationships, whilst being mindful that for many young people, this ideal is not their home experience.

- The content of *evaluate... informing choice* presentations will be stimulating, challenging and informative, encouraging the development of knowledge, attitudes and values that will lead to informed decision-making. This education will:

- provide information and facts about smoking, drugs, alcohol, solvents, pregnancy, *contraception*, Sexually Transmitted Infections including HIV & AIDS and related issues

- develop personal and social skills including negotiation, assertiveness, *self-esteem*

- consider issues focused on relationships, rights, responsibilities and choices.

An evaluate team works within the bounds of an individual school's policy for Sex & Relationship Education, current Department for Education & Skills guidance on Sex & Relationship Education, and the Law relating to sexual activity...

CARE helps children develop their own values

The first thing that we should note is the moral framework upon which CARE's sex education programme is built. CARE says that it aims to provide schoolchildren and young people with a secure and safe environment in which *to develop their own values*. CARE is making it crystal clear that its programme does not teach biblical standards with regard to sexual conduct, but that it helps children and young people develop their owns values to guide their sexual decisions.

CARE's approach is in line with Government policy, expressed in the leaflet *Talking to Your Teenager about Sex and Relationships*, which persuades parents not to offer their children moral guidance, but to help them develop their own values. The Government's leaflet gives parents this advice: 'Discussing your values with your teenagers will help them to form their own. Remember, though, that trying to convince them of what's right and wrong may discourage them from being open.' Simon Calvert of the Christian Institute commented on the leaflet: 'The idea that the government is telling families not to pass on their values is outrageous. Preserving children's innocence is a worthy goal. We would like to see more of that kind of language rather than this amoral approach where parents are encouraged to present their children with a smorgasbord of sexual activities and leave them to make up their own minds.'[3]

To grasp the significance of CARE's teaching we need to understand the influence of Friedrich Nietzsche, the philosopher who opposed the Christian faith with unbridled fury. In *Lessons in Depravity* I wrote:

> The ideas that flowed from Nietzsche's atheistic philosophy promoted the notion that there is no objective truth, and, therefore, no absolute moral standards—the concepts of right and wrong have been discarded, and no act is intrinsically evil. His thinking introduced the idea that each person is free to decide their own truth and their own morality. This philosophy opened the gateway for the sexual revolution. Having removed the absolute moral laws of the Bible, people were free to decide their own values, to set their own standards. Having asserted that God was dead, morality was also dead, and so were the biblical virtues of modesty, chastity and fidelity. Man was now free to make his own arrangements for sexual conduct. The sexual revolutionaries, following Nietzsche's atheistic philosophy, encouraged the idea that people, and even children, are free to develop their own set of sexual values, without regard to an absolute moral standard.[4]

CARE's sex education programme, in line with Nietzsche's godless philosophy, teaches children *to develop their own values* without reference to the absolutes of God's moral law. Yet Scripture tells of a time of moral anarchy in Israel when everyone did what was right in their own eyes (Judges 21:25). Wisdom literature warns: 'There is a way that seems right to a man, but its end is the way of death' (Proverbs 14:12). Therefore, 'lean not on your own understanding; in all your ways acknowledge him, and he shall direct your paths. Do not be wise in your own eyes; fear the Lord and depart from evil' (Proverbs 3: 5-7). But CARE has chosen not to teach biblical standards of conduct, for it prefers to help children develop their own values. The outcome of CARE's approach is moral anarchy that opens the gateway to sexual immorality.

The second point to note is that CARE's sex education policy is designed to work within the bounds of the Government's guidance on Sex & Relationship Education (SRE). The Government's report, *Teenage Pregnancy* (1999), as we saw in chapter 3, warns of the error of moralising. According to the Government, there is no point in teaching biblical moral standards to young people for they will simply make up their own minds. Any attempt to introduce a moral dimension into the discussion on sexual conduct is potentially harmful, for 'moralising' makes children less likely to make the right decision.[5]

We must understand that CARE's approach is entirely consistent with Government policy. Indeed, CARE's prayer guide acknowledges that their sex education programme complements the national curriculum for SRE.[6] In effect CARE has become simply another agency for delivering the Government's sex education programme.

In line with the Government's approach, a key objective of CARE's *evaluate* programme is to help schoolchildren make healthy *informed choices* about their sexual behaviour. The dogma of informed choice is discussed in chapter 8. CARE also follows the Government's position on the importance of *self-esteem* in helping children to make healthy sexual choices. This issue is discussed in chapter 10.

Delaying sexual experience

CARE's policy aims to 'support young people in delaying sexual experience until a committed relationship, ideally marriage'. According to this guidance the essential moral requirement for a sexual experience is a 'committed relationship'. Marriage, while an ideal, is not an essential moral requirement. The implication of this teaching is that it is morally acceptable, in CARE's eyes, for a young couple who are 'committed' to each other to enter a sexual relationship, even if they are not married.

Many young people in a 'committed relationship' will use this advice as a justification to start a sexual relationship. They will rationalise their decision by reasoning that, following CARE's advice, they only became sexually active once they both felt 'committed' to each other. How many young women are deceived by a boyfriend who declares 'everlasting commitment' in order to entice her into a sexual relationship? And how many young couples, having followed this advice, enter into a 'committed' cohabiting relationship, only for it to end after a year or two? CARE is implanting into the minds of young people the idea that the Christian faith permits a couple in a 'committed relationship' to become sexually active whether or not they are married. This teaching encourages fornication and is in direct opposition to Scripture.

CARE's policy on condom education

The sex education industry revolves around the condom. The key 'fact' promoted by sex educators is that condoms provide 'all-in-one' protection against pregnancy and STIs. The aim of sex education, therefore, is to teach children how to use condoms consistently and correctly.

The high profile media campaign around the poster 'Want Respect: Use a Condom', promoted by the Government's Teenage Pregnancy Unit, is symbolic of the sex education industry. The slogan of Marie Stopes International, a leading provider of sexual health services in the UK, is 'Cover the World with Condoms'. Brook's poster campaign, 'Have fun, be careful', reminded young people to use condoms over the festive season. Brook's leaflet, *The cool lovers guide to slick condom use*, shows teenagers how to use a condom correctly.

Here is CARE's policy on condoms which has been downloaded from the *evaluate* website:

> As the *evaluate* programme provides education about choices available to people in the light of HIV & AIDS and other sexually transmitted infections, this will *include education about condom use*. The *evaluate* programme does not promote the exclusive use of condoms as the only choice for young people with regard to sexual behaviour. Rather, *evaluate* educators provide such education in accordance with the World Health Organisation position, which is 'abstinence and fidelity between uninfected partners and safer sex can prevent the transmission of HIV. *Safer sex includes non-penetrative sex and sex using condoms.*' Evaluate educators do not give out condoms in schools nor are condom demonstrators part of these demonstrations [my italics].

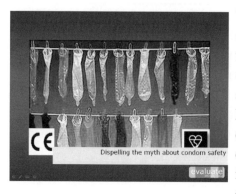

Dispelling the myth about condom safety

While condoms are not presented as the only choice, *evaluate* educators present them as an option for children to consider as they think about protecting themselves from HIV and other STIs. CARE is careful to say that *evaluate* educators do not give out condoms in schools and do not use a condom demonstrator. Nevertheless, *evaluate* educators have no reservations about showing children a picture of condoms draped from a clothes line (picture above). They also present a cartoon image of the condom as a friendly, smiling face (page 59, also page 112). Undoubtedly, teaching children about condoms is central to CARE's message.

CARE and the World Health Organisation (WHO)

CARE's condom education is based on the WHO policy statement on Condoms and HIV Prevention (July 2004), which asserts that 'condoms are an integral and essential part of comprehensive prevention and care programmes, and their promotion must be accelerated... Condoms are a key component of combination prevention strategies individuals can choose at different times in their lives to reduce their risks of sexual exposure to HIV. These include delay of sexual initiation, abstinence, being safer by being faithful to one's partner when both partners are uninfected and consistently faithful, reducing the number of sexual partners, and correct and consistent use of condoms.'[7] Based on this guidance, CARE's *evaluate* programme promotes the ABC model of sex education among schoolchildren (see picture page 60).

CARE's sex educators, in accordance with the WHO position, teach that '...safer sex can prevent the transmission of HIV. Safer sex includes *non-penetrative sex* [my italics] and sex using condoms.' The reason for teaching children about *non-penetrative sex* (that is, oral sex, anal sex and mutual masturbation) is the belief that, if children are taught the pleasures of *non-penetrative sex*, they will be less likely to indulge in vaginal sex, thereby reducing the risk of teenage pregnancy.

The 'A Pause' sex education programme of Exeter University is a keen exponent of non-penetrative sex. According to the programme director, John Rees, it is about getting 14 and 15-year-olds to think about stages of intimacy that do not involve penetrative sex, with its risks of pregnancy and infection.[8] He added: 'It's about saying to them.

CARE's cartoon of a friendly condom from an *evaluate* presentation

"You can hold hands, you can kiss and cuddle", it may even get as far as something like oral sex or even mutual masturbation.'[9] The underlying aim is to encourage school pupils to think about oral and anal sex, and mutual masturbation as alternatives to sexual intercourse.

Condom education without morality

The reason CARE teaches children how to use condoms is so that if they make an informed choice to have sex they are able to 'protect' themselves. Does CARE's condom education encourage lust? Does it lead children into sexual temptation? Does the idea of 'safer sex' open the gateway to sexual immorality? Is it right to teach children about non-penetrative sex? The answer to these questions is obvious, for teaching children about condoms is likely to inflame sexual lust. Yet *evaluate* educators appear to be unconcerned that they are inculcating into the minds of other people's children the possibility of 'safer sex'—the idea of risk free sex. *Evaluate* educators claim to 'feel that they are part of what God is doing to change young people's lives – and the way society thinks about sexuality'.[10] CARE's supporters are being asked to accept that teaching children how to use condoms is part of God's plan to change young people's lives.

CARE's sex educators need to ask themselves whether teaching children about condoms is causing them to fall into sin. Our Lord said, 'Whoever causes one of these little ones who believe in me to fall into

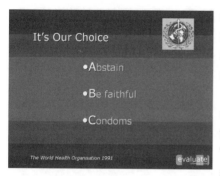

sin, it would be better for him if a millstone were hung around his neck, and he were thrown into the sea' (Mark 9:42).

The most disturbing aspect of CARE's sex education policy is that it is devoid of moral guidance. There is no reference to biblical standards of sexual conduct; there is no attempt to teach children that certain types of sexual behaviour are wrong. The concept of sexual purity, which lies at the heart of Christian teaching, is simply ignored. The biblical virtues of modesty, self-control and chastity are disregarded. By helping children to develop their own values CARE is saying to them that God's moral law is irrelevant. CARE is inculcating into the minds of children a godless philosophy that opens the gateway to sexual immorality. It does not take much insight to see that CARE's amoral sex education is no different from that delivered by the FPA, Brook and the Government's sexual health strategy.

While CARE happily accepts the WHO as an authority on sexual behaviour, in doing so it has denied the God of Scripture. The reason that CARE's sex educators turn to the WHO for guidance on condom education is because they have rejected the moral law of God. But let CARE be warned that the Holy God, who loves righteousness and hates evil, will call them to account for what they are doing in his name.

(Endnotes)

1 BBC online, News channel, 'Expert warns of sex disease crisis', Tuesday, 15 April 2003
2 Evaluate website, Teachers page, Sex or no sex? that is the question!
3 *Times* online, *The Sunday Times*, 22 February 2009, Parents told: avoid morality in sex lessons
4 ES Williams, *Lessons in Depravity*, Belmont House Publishing, 2003, p58
5 *Teenage pregnancy*, HMSO, London, June 1999, p90
6 CARE's Prayer Guide, April to August 2008, p20
7 Position Statement on Condoms and HIV Prevention July 2004, Condom use is a critical element in a comprehensive, effective and sustainable approach to HIV prevention and treatment. WHO, UNAIDS, UNFPA
8 BCC News website, 21 February 2003, Sex lessons 'go too far'
9 Times Educational Supplement website, taken from Breaking News, 21 February 2003, Under-16s health course 'should have avoided the mention of oral sex'
10 *CARE Today*, Issue 12, Winter 2006, page 8

6

CARE's advice on sexual behaviour

The *evaluate* programme consists of three multimedia presentations aimed at different age groups in secondary schools. The presentation *This Is Your Life!* is for children aged 11 to 13 and focuses on their worth as unique and special individuals. Delivered to large audiences of up to 150 students, it makes use of role play, group work and teaches assertiveness skills, as well as building self-esteem. The effect of drugs and alcohol on decision making is explored. The qualities of friendship are considered and a lively quiz revisits and consolidates information given throughout the presentation.

The presentation *Sex – How Safe?* is for children aged 13 to 15 and *Just The One!* is for those aged 15 to 18. These presentations build further layers of information and enable students, by discussion in small groups, to examine the nature of lasting relationships, commitment, trust and faithfulness. Media pressures are examined, and the message behind popular music, magazines and advertising is explored, and risk taking behaviour is considered.

A feature of CARE's sex education programme is that it includes a number of quizzes for children and young people. Those who attend a presentation are invited to take part in these quizzes, which are available on the CARE *evaluate* website. In this chapter we analyse the content of CARE's quizzes. This will help us to understand the messages that CARE's sex educators are imparting to children. Once again, we should remind ourselves that the issue at stake is whether CARE's teaching is consistent with the Christian faith. As Christians, we know that Scripture emphasises sexual purity. 'Who may ascend into the hill of the Lord? Or who may stand in his holy place? He who has clean hands and a pure heart' (Psalm 24:3-4).

As we go through a selection of questions we need to consider the underlying purpose of each quiz. What information are the questions seeking to reinforce in the minds of those who take part?

Questions for children aged 11-13

The first quiz comes from *This Is Your Life!* aimed at children aged 11 to 13 and includes a question on sexually transmitted infections (STIs). Evidently *evaluate* sex educators believe that children need to know about diseases that are transmitted by sexual intercourse. Here is the question:

Which is the most common STI in the UK?

A HIV;

B Syphilis;

C Chlamydia;

D Gonorrhoea;

E Genital warts.

Answer: The most common STI in the UK is chlamydia, with genital warts being the next highest.

The implication of this question is that 11-year-olds should have a rather detailed knowledge of the incidence of STIs. But how does an innocent child benefit from this knowledge? Does the mind of an 11-year-old really need to come to terms with the idea of genital warts, syphilis and gonorrhoea? Does an innocent young girl need to be thinking about the frequency of chlamydia and HIV? What kind of organisation wants to impart this morbid information to children?

We heard in chapter 3 that the British Humanist Association says that good sex education would teach about the importance of the family, 'recognising that increasingly in today's society, the family can take many forms, and that same sex civil partnerships are now recognised in law alongside heterosexual marriage'. We have also seen that the

Bible teaches that a new family is created at the marriage of a man and a woman. *This Is Your Life!* shows a picture entitled 'family' that is represented by six groups of people. Look carefully at each group. What do they say about the family? CARE should explain what the group of two women with a young boy means in the context of the family. And what is the meaning of the smallest group in the background? The reader can judge for themselves whether CARE's teaching about the family is consistent with biblical truth.

Questions for children aged 13-15

The next quiz is based on the presentation *Sex – How Safe?* aimed at 13 to 15-year-olds. Here we should remember that the age of sexual consent is 16—it is unlawful for a man to have sexual intercourse with a girl before her sixteenth birthday. Once again the quiz will give us a good idea of the information that CARE wishes to reinforce in the minds of children. Here is a selection of questions from the quiz—the whole quiz can be viewed online:

> *Can a girl get pregnant if she has sex standing up?* Answer is YES.
> Gravity won't help, those sperm know where they are going!

Are two condoms better than one? Answer is NO. The opposite! Two are weaker! Using two can damage the condom.

Can a girl get pregnant if she jumps up and down after sex? Answer is yes... and she would look rather odd! Going to the loo after sex doesn't help either!

Is using a condom safe sex? Answer is no... it is safeR sex – not completely safe! There are many methods of contraception available – the pill, diaphragm or cap, intra-uterine device or coil, injections, implants, patch, spermicidal preparations, male and female condoms, and natural methods such as Persona. Although many are very effective, no method is 100% safe. Also, and this is very important, ONLY condoms provide a waterproof barrier to provide protection from sexually transmitted infections.

Can a girl get pregnant if the boy withdraws before he ejaculates? Answer is yes. Pre-ejaculatory fluid can be released during sex which does contain sperm. The boy may not even realise it has been released.

Can a girl get pregnant if she misses a couple of pills out of a packet? Answer is yes. All pills must be taken. The worst ones to miss are the last one out of the packet or the first one from the next packet. If she does forget to take a pill, it's OK if she remembers within 12 hours; she can still take it. But if it is longer than that, they would need to use condoms for 7 days and then start a new packet of pills.

Is it unhealthy for a boy not to have sex? Answer is no. Sperm will dissolve into his body – WHATEVER HE TRIES TO SAY!!

What is so objectionable about this quiz is that it seeks to trivialize sexual immorality among children. Note the number of questions that are embellished with an exclamation mark. Author F. Scott Fitzgerald comments: 'Cut out all those exclamation marks. An exclamation mark is like laughing at your own jokes.' CARE, with its eight exclamation marks, wants children to join with them in laughing about questions that trivialize sex. Yet Scripture warns that there must not be even a hint of sexual immorality, or of any kind of impurity, because these are improper for God's holy people (Ephesians 5:3).

Notice how CARE makes light of sexual immorality. *Can a girl get pregnant if she jumps up and down after sex?* The answer is yes... and she would look rather odd! So it's really quite funny to think of a girl jumping up and down after sex. We can all have a good laugh about that. Why take it so seriously, it's just a bit of fun, and the reason she jumps up and down is because her boyfriend did not use a condom. CARE does not warn that sexual immorality is wrong—there is no warning that the young girl has sinned against her own body and will bear the consequences of her sin (1 Corinthians 6:18).

And what is the point of asking a 13-year-old girl if she can get pregnant if she has sex standing up? Has such a thought entered the mind of the average 13-year-old child?

Behind CARE's questions is an assumption that most children, even 13-year-olds, are going to be sexually active anyway and therefore they all need a detailed knowledge of sex, contraception and STIs. But most 13-year-olds have no intention of becoming sexually active and many are deeply upset by the explicit and crude messages of the *evaluate* educators that treat sex as a subject that can be joked about and discussed openly. Their childhood innocence and natural modesty is offended.

And what is CARE's very important message about sex? For children to know 'that ONLY condoms provide a waterproof barrier to provide protection from sexually transmitted infections'. The very important message of the Christian faith, on the other hand, is to teach children the value of self-control and to warn them to 'abstain from fleshly lusts which war against the soul' (1 Peter 2:11).

Questions for 15 to 18-year-olds

There are three quizzes based on CARE's *Just the One!* presentation—the first focuses on STIs, the second on condoms and the third on contraception. Here is a selection of questions from the contraception quiz:

> *In the UK, some types of contraception incur a prescription charge?*
> Answer is: False. All contraceptives are free if obtained via a doctor
> or nurse. However, emergency contraception may also be purchased

for approximately £25 by women of 16 years old via a pharmacist who has undergone specific training and who works to specific guidelines (a Patient Group Directive). Condoms may be purchased at various outlets.

After seeing a person under 16 years of age, doctors and nurses have a duty to tell parents and carers what happened, and let them look at the records. Answer is: False. However, under the Fraser Guidelines, doctors and nurses should encourage the teenager to talk with a parent or carer.

An internal examination is usually necessary before the contraceptive pill can be prescribed for the first time. Answer is: False. The doctor or nurse will ask questions about personal and family history, and measure blood pressure and weight.

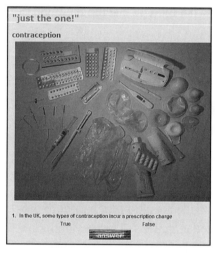

"just the one!"
contraception

1. In the UK, some types of contraception incur a prescription charge
   True   False
   answer

After having unprotected sex a woman has 48 hours – 2 days – to get emergency contraception (the morning-after pill). Answer is: False. Emergency contraception is licensed for use for 72 hours after unprotected sex, and will have some effect beyond this time. An IUD (coil) may be fitted up to 5 days after unprotected sex, or up to 5 days after earliest possible ovulation.

A woman has to wait at least 2 weeks after sex for a pregnancy test to give a reliable result. Answer is: True. She needs to wait 3 weeks after sex to be sure of a negative result.

It's OK to use KY jelly with condoms to aid lubrication. Answer is: True. Oil-based lubricants may cause rubber (latex) to perish so should not be used with condoms, but there is no concern with water-based lubricants such as KY jelly.

The injectable contraceptive Depo-Provera can be dangerous if it stops the periods. Answer is: False. Depo-Provera frequently stops the periods, which many women appreciate, and which is not dangerous.

[This information is misleading for it suggests to schoolgirls and young women that Depo-Provera is a safe drug. Yet the USA Food and Drug Administration (FDA), together with the manufacturer of Depo-Provera (Pfizer), have issued the following 'black box' warning because of the significant health risks associated with the drug:

'Women who use Depo-Provera Contraceptive Injection may lose significant bone mineral density. Bone loss is greater with increasing duration of use and may not be completely reversible.'

The injection, 'reduces serum oestrogen levels and is associated with significant loss of bone mineral density as bone metabolism accommodates to a lower oestrogen level. This loss of bone mineral density is of particular concern during adolescence and early adulthood, a critical period of bone accretion.'[1]

According to the manufacturer's guide: 'The loss of calcium may increase your risk of osteoporosis and broken bones, particularly after your menopause.'[2]

So there is a real danger that the loss of bone mineral density during adolescence and early adulthood may not be reversible and leads to an increased risk of osteoporosis. It seems that CARE is so blinded by its commitment to the contraceptive culture that it is prepared to promote a false view of Depo-Provera among schoolchildren and young people.]

Here is a selection of questions from the condom quiz:

What are condoms made of? Answer is: Latex rubber or polyurethane.

What should you check for on a packet of condoms? Answer is: Expiry date, BSI Kitemark and European CE mark, Packet intact.

Where should condoms be kept? Answer is: Cool dry place, out of direct sunlight.

When should the condom be put on? Answer is: Once penis is erect but before any genital contact.

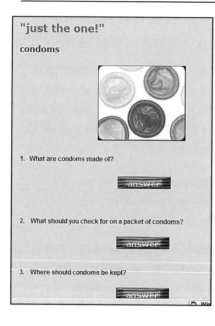

"just the one!"

condoms

1. What are condoms made of?

answer

2. What should you check for on a packet of condoms?

answer

3. Where should condoms be kept?

answer

How many times can a condom be used? Answer is: Only once!

Does using two condoms at a time make them stronger or safer? Answer is: No, more likely to split because more friction.

What type of lubricant can be used with a condom? Answer is: Water-based lubricants such as KY Jelly. NOT oil-based lubricants, e.g. baby oil, vaseline as they weaken the latex.

How should a condom be disposed of? Answer is: Wrap in a paper tissue and put in a bin. NOT down the toilet!

Are condoms containing spermicide better? Answer is: No, because spermicide on condoms (nonoxynol) can irritate the vaginal wall and encourage infection so there's a higher risk of STIs.

What should be considered if a condom splits? Answer is: Emergency contraception, Testing for STIs.

CARE's advice on sexual behaviour

The above questions give us a good idea what CARE's *evaluate* educators are teaching children and young people about sex, and the information they want to consolidate in their young minds. They are making sure children know that 'all contraceptives are free if obtained via a doctor or nurse'. They also make sure under-age children know that their parents will not find out that they are using contraceptives for, 'after seeing a person under 16 years of age' the doctor or nurse supplying the contraceptives will not tell their parents about the visit. This raises the important question – does CARE actually support the Government's policy of providing under-age children with free contraception without their parents' knowledge or consent?

We have seen that CARE expects children and young people to know that condoms are made of latex and that before using a condom they should check the expiry date, BSI Kitemark and European CE mark. And CARE advises young people to keep their condoms in a 'cool dry place, out of direct sunlight'. And when they decide to have sex, the time to put a condom on their partner is '...before any genital contact'. And young people must remember to use a condom just once and not use two condoms at one time because two are 'more likely to split because more friction'.

And to help make a young woman's sex life as enjoyable as possible, CARE advises her to use a water-based lubricant. And she must not use a condom with spermicide because it 'can irritate the vaginal wall and encourage infection so there's a higher risk of STIs'. CARE reminds young people that when they are finished having sex, they should wrap the condom in a paper tissue and put it in a bin, and not down the toilet. And if a young woman has bad luck and the condom splits then she needs to consider using emergency contraception and getting herself checked out for STIs.

CARE also makes sure that schoolgirls know all the details about emergency contraception—even to the point of correcting those who think that emergency contraception can only be used within 48 hours of the event. CARE informs them that they can use emergency contraception up to 72 hours after 'unprotected' sex, and 16-year-olds can purchase emergency contraception from a pharmacist.

Notice again that CARE's teaching is not only devoid of moral content, but that it gives advice to help young people enjoy having sex. CARE even makes sure that schoolchildren contemplating sex know that 'It's OK to use KY jelly with condoms to aid lubrication.' Here we should note that the website of Marie Stopes International, aimed at young people, discusses different 'lubes' and makes it clear that 'KY jelly gets our vote'. Likewise, Brook advises young people that 'taking things slowly and using extra lubrication, like KY jelly' can help them enjoy sex.[3] So CARE's teaching on lubrication is the same as that of Marie Stopes and Brook.

CARE's sex quizzes show a total disregard for the moral conventions that are held by most people in British society. Indeed, most people would be appalled at the thought that a Christian organisation is teaching schoolchildren how to use and dispose of condoms.

What image of the Christian faith do these quizzes create in the minds of teachers and schoolchildren? Are they helpful in building up those who take part? Do they impart grace to the hearers? On the contrary, they introduce children and young people to the world of licentious sexual ideas that trivialize sexual immorality. The fact that a Christian organisation takes these salacious quizzes into the school classroom is deeply damaging to the witness of the Church. But few people understand the hypocrisy behind CARE's sex education programme. Lyndon Bowring's news letter (November 2008) presents this face to its supporters:

> I know you share our deep concern for our children's and grandchildren's welfare. Growing up in today's hedonistic, highly sexualised culture is not easy, even for them. Life for young people has become a moral minefield. Alongside local churches and other Christian organisations CARE is committed to making a Christian difference for the sake of the future in the whole area of sexuality.

Indeed. Are these quizzes, with their focus on contraception, STIs and KY jelly, making a Christian difference in the whole area of sexuality? Lyndon Bowring needs to open his eyes to the fact that CARE's salacious sex quizzes are contributing to the sexualisation of children.

Despite its smooth, charming public face, behind its façade CARE's teaching is an abomination—it is linking the Church of Christ with the amoral teaching of the sex education industry.

(Endnotes)

1 Product warning from Pfizer, Healthcare Organisation Leader, 18 November 2004
2 Pharmacia & Upjohn, Division of Pfizer, Patient information, Risk of using Depo-Provera, Revised October 2004
3 Brook website, Questions, Sex and relationships

7

Sex surveys

It is widely known that several teenager magazines contain sexually explicit material.[1] Sue Palmer, an educational consultant and author of *Toxic Childhood* (2006) has said, 'The reality is that children as young as 10 read these magazines, and what they are being exposed to is often horrific and inappropriate. The very blatantly sexual ethos expressed in them is becoming normalized among young girls. Then we wonder why we have such high teenage pregnancy rates and a booming ladette culture.'[2] The Government's consumer watchdog, Consumer Focus, believes that magazines like *Bliss* could be responsible for the early sexualisation of young readers.

CARE's prayer guidance (January 2009) asks its supporters to pray about the issue of teenage magazines:

> Ask God to give wisdom to parents who want their families to experience the innocent joys of childhood, without being confronted with inappropriate images, words and music. Help them to find a balance between preparing their children for the wider world and protecting them from harm. Pray about music, videos and magazines that refer very explicitly and casually to sex. These can encourage many young people to become sexually active, resulting in health and social problems, emotional distress, and unwanted pregnancies.[3]

CARE's prayer is that children should experience the innocent joys of childhood without being confronted with inappropriate images. CARE understands that teenage magazines that refer to explicit sex may encourage young people to become sexually active, resulting in health, social and emotional problems. Supporters are encouraged to believe that CARE stands opposed to the indecent content of these magazines.

The Bliss sex survey

Most parents know that the highly sexualised contents of *Bliss* are unsuitable for young girls. Parents concerned about the moral welfare of their teenage daughter would surely warn her against reading such provocative, explicit material. It seems amazing, then, that CARE's *evaluate* website has chosen to report the sensational findings of an online sex survey done by *Bliss*, and even to use the findings as a justification for its sex education programme. Here is what young people surfing CARE's *evaluate* website will read:

> More recently, in breaking news of a survey done in *Bliss* magazine, the *Telegraph* informed us that almost a quarter of 14-year-old girls claim to have had sex and say they have had an average of three partners. Among those who said they had had sex, 65% admitted to unprotected sex and 45% say they had a one-night stand…

> It is against this backdrop that a new multimedia Sex & Relationship Education programme called *evaluate… informing choice* has been developed. If the results of this survey are a true representation, and the UK's shamefully high rates of unintended teenage pregnancy and sexually transmitted infections seem to bear this out, then there is indeed much to do to turn the tide. The survey concludes that there is a desperate need among young people for accurate and reliable information on sex

> and relationships so that they can make informed choices about when they are ready to have sex and to resist peer pressure…

Predictably, the 'survey' of two thousand *Bliss* readers produced sensational newspaper headlines, such as, 'A quarter of girls aged 14 claim to have sex with several partners' (*The Daily Telegraph*) and 'One fifth of teenage girls are sexually active by 14' (*Independent*).[4] As expected *Bliss* received a great deal of publicity for its sex survey which provided useful ammunition for those who promote the idea that young people need even more sex education.

But how reliable are the findings of the *Bliss* online survey? Obviously those who responded to a survey conducted by a girlie magazine are a highly selective group and certainly not representative of teenagers. Respondents are a subset of *Bliss* readership who have something to say about sex. Those who have not had under-age sex were less likely to participate, and those who took part may well have exaggerated their sexual adventures. Even the FPA acknowledged that the 'study' was biased and flawed.

Professor Kaye Wellings, the principal investigator of the National Survey of Sexual Attitudes and Lifestyles in 2000, commented: '*Bliss* is quite an upfront magazine sexually, so girls who buy it are not representative of girls in general and readers who reply to a survey are not representative of *Bliss* readers. If you choose to fill in a form, you may be more sexually confident.'[5] According to Professor Wellings the National Survey showed that 13% of 14-year-olds had had sex—not the shocking 25% as claimed by *Bliss*.

So the findings reported by *Bliss* are little more than sensational propaganda used to promote a campaign for more sex education and greater condom distribution. Why does CARE want to promote this flawed survey? By quoting the findings, CARE is giving *Bliss* magazine credibility in the eyes of schoolchildren.

The BareAll06 sex survey

In 2006 the BBC, MTV and condom manufacturer, Durex, jointly conducted a sex survey which they entitled *BareAll06*. The Managing Director of Durex UK explained the purpose of the survey, 'Durex will be giving half a million condoms to the *BareAll06* campaign; these will be distributed at festivals and through listener giveaways during the summer. This supports our overall, ongoing commitment to improving the sexual health of the nation. Condoms are the only form of contraception to protect against STIs and unplanned pregnancies and by partnering with organisations with such kudos as Radio 1, 1Xtra and MTV, we're sure that we'll hit the right audiences throughout the length of the campaign.'[6]

The week-long *BareAll06* campaign was fronted by two popular DJs who offered listeners the chance to win an exclusive Safer Sex Sack con-

taining condoms, a limited edition condom holder, T-shirt with a condom pocket and other safer sex goodies. Young people were asked why safer sex messages are not getting through, and what they would need to be better informed about safer sex. In August 2006, the results of *BareAll06* were announced across MTV, Radio 1 and 1Xtra via special TV and radio programming.[7]

Despite clear evidence that the so-called survey was simply part of a campaign to promote condoms among young people and to engage in salacious talk, CARE chose to publicize the results. Here is the BBC news item (15 August 06) quoted on CARE's website:

'Nearly a third of 16 to 24-year-olds lost their virginity below the age of consent, a survey has suggested. The BBC Radio 1 poll also suggested 43% of young people had had at least five sexual partners with one in five having more than 10. Over half (57%) claimed to have had a one-night stand. But many of the youngsters, who made up two-thirds of the 29,623 who responded to the online poll, said they did not always use condoms with new partners...

The survey, carried out in conjunction with BBC, 1Xtra, Durex and MTV, also revealed deficiencies in young people's sex education. One in 10 claimed to have had no sex education at school, while three quarters said they only learned the basics...

A spokesman for Brook, the sexual health charity for young people, said: 'In many respects these findings are not surprising, but they are still worrying. What it shows is how important it is to provide young people with good sexual education. But unfortunately much of the teaching in schools is too biologically-based.'

Vicky Field of the HIV charity, Terrence Higgins Trust, agreed. She said: 'Without changes in the way we talk to young people about sex, rates of sexually transmitted infections will continue to increase dramatically...'

Story from BBC NEWS published 13/8/06. Survey BareAll06, an online poll supported by the Department of Health.

Unreliable evidence

It is surprising that CARE appears to be unaware of the methodological problems which make the findings of the *Bliss* and *BareAll06* surveys unreliable and misleading. As a Christian *research* organisation it should know better than to take the findings of these surveys at face value. But CARE seems to be unconcerned that the results are little more than propaganda to promote the idea that children and young people are sexually ignorant, and therefore in desperate need of more sex education.

Equally disturbing is the fact that CARE is happy to publish the comments of spokesmen from Brook and Terrence Higgins Trust without qualification or comment. Clearly the purpose of their comments is to support the argument that children need more sex education. Moreover, CARE quotes the BBC's description of Brook as a sexual health charity for young people without qualification or comment. Yet we have seen that Brook, an organisation that specialises in supplying contraceptives to under-age children, is fundamentally opposed to the biblical view of sexual conduct. The chairman of Brook, Evelyn Asante-Mensah, said she would love to see our society become much more open in talking about sex and sexuality. 'A more open society, communicating about sex in a non-judgmental way would certainly be my vision of the future – and one where people were empowered to talk more openly about lesbian sex, too. How can any of us begin to explore what we like and don't like sexually if we feel impeded from talking to one another about sex?'[8]

CARE justifies its sex education programme

What is CARE's motivation in quoting these unreliable sex surveys? The answer is not difficult to find for CARE freely admits that it is against the backdrop of the *Bliss* survey that its 'new multimedia Sex & Relationship Education programme called *evaluate... informing choice* has been developed'. CARE argues that 'if the results of this survey are a true representation, and the UK's shamefully high rates of unintended teenage pregnancy and sexually transmitted infections seem to bear this out, then there is indeed much to do to turn the tide'. So CARE is ready to accept the findings of the *Bliss* survey as a true representation of the situation in the UK. This leads to the conclusion that 'there is a desperate need among young people for accurate and reliable information on sex and relationships so that they can make informed choices about when they are ready to have sex and to resist peer pressure'. So the way to turn the tide, in the eyes of CARE, is not to teach young people God's plan for sexual conduct, but to give them more sex education.

The *BareAll06* survey is also supposed to have 'revealed deficiencies in young people's sex education'. And CARE quotes Brook's interpretation that the findings show 'how important it is to provide young people with good sex education'. So the *evaluate* website refers to two dubious surveys to support its case that young people are sexually ignorant and in desperate need of sex education.

Such is the moral bankruptcy of CARE that it accepts the 'wisdom' of two sex surveys, one conducted by a salacious teenage magazine and the other by a condom manufacturer, as the justification for its *evaluate* sex education project. This is an important point for those who support CARE to understand—the justification for CARE's sex education programme comes not from Scripture but from the spirit of the age.

Scripture is clear that God's people should not follow the wisdom of man. 'Woe to the rebellious children,' says the Lord, 'Who take counsel, but not of me, and who devise plans, but not of my Spirit, that they may add sin to sin; who walk to go down to Egypt, and have not asked my advice, to strengthen themselves in the strength of Pharaoh, and to trust in the shadow of Egypt! Therefore the strength of Pharaoh shall be your shame' (Isaiah 30:1). The shame of CARE, an organisation that claims to be Christian, is that it has used the counsel of *Bliss* magazine and the *BareAll06* survey as a justification for its sex education programme.

(Endnotes)

1 *The Sunday Telegraph*, 15 March 2009, 'The top-shelf teen magazines', Roya Nikkhah,
2 Ibid.
3 CARE's prayer guide, January to April 2009, Teenage sexuality, 12 and 13 January 2009
4 www.drpetra.co.uk/blog/?p=65
5 *The Daily Telegraph*, 24 March 2005, 'A quarter of girls aged 14 claim to have had sex with several partners', Catriona Davies
6 BBC Press Releases, BareAll06 – Radio 1, 1Xtra and MTV talk to young people about safer sex, Category: Radio 1; 1Xtra, Date: 23.05.2006
7 Ibid.
8 SHINE, Issue 10, August 2007, an interview with… In this issue we speak to Evelyn Asante-Mensah, OBE, Chair of Brook

The dogma of informed choice

The title of CARE's sex education programme, *evaluate… informing choice*, is well chosen for it expresses CARE's deep commitment to the concept of informed choice. *CARE Today* tells how a team from the *evaluate* programme presented their multimedia package to the Royal

Ballet School in Richmond Park, teaching more than 120 students how to make healthy, informed decisions about relationships.[1] In this chapter we shall see that both CARE's sex education programme and its crisis pregnancy counselling ministry aim to empower individuals to make truly informed decisions with regard to the difficult moral choices that they face.

CARE promotes informed choice

CARE's website explains that the *evaluate* project 'aims to impact young people's moral values and attitudes to sex by supporting them in making informed choices'.[2] A key objective of CARE's sex education policy, as we saw in chapter 5, is to 'empower, equip and enable young people to make healthy informed choices'. At the core of the *evaluate* project lies the belief that every young person is unique and capable of making healthy choices. The claim is that empowering young people to make informed choices will change their attitude to sex and impact their moral values.

Referring to the findings of the sex survey done by *Bliss* magazine, discussed in chapter 7, the *evaluate* website concludes 'that there is a desperate need among young people for accurate and reliable information on sex and relationships so that they can make informed choices about when they are ready to have sex and to resist peer pressure'.[3] CARE's prayer guide says: 'Ask God to continue blessing CARE's volunteer teams of Christian educators presenting the 'evaluate' sex and relationship education programme. Pray that it will empower young people to make healthy informed decisions, to delay sexual experience and have real hope for a future that will be safe and fulfilled.'[4]

CARE's video *Make Love Last*, discussed in chapter 2, helps young people come to a balanced and sound decision about their sexual behaviour. 'Young people have the right and need to examine the major options on offer. Without this opportunity they cannot make an informed choice.'[5] The Northern Ireland sex education programme, Love for Life, is also committed to the informed choice agenda. Its website entitled 'Icebergs and Babies' is 'here for you to use, enjoy and to help you make informed and mature sexual health choices – choices that will effect you now and in your future'.[6]

Turning to crisis pregnancy counselling, we see that the concept of informed choice is central to CARE's network of clinics scattered around the UK. CARE's pregnancy counsellors are trained in non-directive counselling, enabling them to help a pregnant woman to discover more clearly how she feels about her situation and to discuss the three options that are open to her—keep the baby, adoption or abortion. The pregnant woman is provided with all the information she needs to make an informed choice between these options.

The CareConfidential website advises a woman with an unwanted pregnancy: 'You need to know the options available to you and you need support to help you through the decision making process. It may feel very urgent to do something right now. Take time to think through the options clearly so that you make an informed decision.'[7] According to CARE's training manual, *Called to Care*, one of the main goals of counselling is to bring a woman 'to the point where she can make a fully informed decision'.[8] CARE Centres Network advises a woman: 'You are entitled to this information so that you and your partner can make an informed choice.'[9]

Evaluate sex educators discuss the issue of unwanted pregnancies. Young women are told that if they have an unwanted pregnancy, then they have three options—keep the baby, abortion and adoption (see picture). A crisis pregnancy counsellor will help them make an informed choice between the options.

So CARE is up front in declaring that its sex education and pregnancy counselling programmes are built on the principle of the informed choice. Its aim is to impact young people's moral values and attitudes to sex and abortion by giving them the information they need to make truly informed decisions. But where does the concept of informed choice come from— the teaching of Scripture or the spirit of this age?

Informed choice in the secular world

Virtually all secular sex education programmes in the UK are built around the concept of the informed choice. While the language of the pro-choice movement may vary, with phrases such as 'informed decision', 'healthy choice', 'responsible decision' and so on being common, the underlying meaning is the same—a young man or young woman is provided with information to enable him or her to make a choice between the various sexual options that are open to them.

The FPA declares that 'if people are to enjoy positive sexual health, they need knowledge and awareness from which to make informed choices, and the confidence to express their sexuality'.[10] The purpose of the FPA 'is to enable people in the UK to make informed choices about sex and to enjoy sexual health'.[11] The Brook mission statement says that it 'exists to enable all young people to make informed choices about their personal and sexual relationships so that they can enjoy their sexuality without harm'.[12] Marie Stopes International is 'committed to providing all the help you need to make informed choices about your health'.[13] The Sex Education Forum claims that children and young people want to learn and practice personal skills which will help them 'to take responsibility for their own and other's sexual health, to access support and help and to make informed choices and decisions regarding their sexual health and emotional well-being'.[14]

The Department of Health's report, *You're Welcome*, offers guidance on sexual health services for young people. 'Young people are offered appropriate information and advice to help them develop their ability to make safe, informed choices. This should include helping them to develop the confidence and skills to delay early sex and resist peer pressure.'[15] The Teenage Pregnancy Unit's innovative campaign 'Want Respect: Use a Condom' aims to encourage teenagers to make informed decisions about sex and reduce pregnancy rates. The review of SRE in schools stresses the importance of young people being given the information they need to make informed choices.[16]

The concept of informed choice is central to pro-choice abortion counselling. The policy of the British Pregnancy Advisory Service is to provide information so that every woman understands all options open to her. 'Choosing whether or not to have an abortion is a significant decision for every woman and *bpas* can provide information to help make an informed decision that is right for her.'[17] The counsellors of Planned Parenthood 'provide information to help women and couples make informed choices'.[18] Brook Advisory Centres believe that 'it is every woman's right to choose an abortion. Women should have access to impartial information and support in order to make an informed choice about their pregnancy.'[19] A Marie Stopes booklet on abortion helps a woman reach an informed decision about the options available to her.[20]

Task Force on Informed Choice

The term informed choice first appeared in family planning literature in the early 1970s when the United States Agency for International Aid (USAID) said that it supported contraceptive programmes that were based on the principle of informed choice.[21] In 1987, the Task Force on Informed Choice, consisting of representatives from 17 organisations working in the field of family planning, developed guidance on how informed choice should be used in programmes that promote contraception.[22] Sponsored by USAID, the Task Force had representation from the United Nations

Population Fund and the International Planned Parenthood Federation (IPPF) among others.

The Task Force defined informed choice as effective access to information on reproductive choices and to the necessary counselling 'to help individuals choose and use an appropriate method of family planning, if desired'.[23] The Task Force claimed that 'the goal of counselling is to have the client arrive at a choice that he/she is satisfied with and, if the choice is to use contraception, to prepare the client to use his/her chosen method effectively'.[24] It concluded that much progress had been made in promoting informed choice and recommended that family planning agencies should develop a training module specifically on informed choice.[25]

The Cairo International Conference on Population and Development (1994) reached a consensus, which involved 179 governments, on a programme of action through 2015: 'The principle of informed free choice is essential to the long-term success of family planning programs.'[26]

During the last two decades the concept of informed choice has become an integral part of virtually all family planning, abortion counselling and sex education programmes worldwide.

The International Planned Parenthood Federation (IPPF)

The IPPF Annual Programme Review says that its commitment 'towards empowering young people to make informed decisions and choices regarding their sexual and reproductive health has been solid and unwavering since the early 1990s'.[27] The underlying principle which guides the work of IPPF is a rights-based approach, with International Human Rights treaties informing the way it works with young people. The IPPF claims that 'youth empowerment, informed choice and practices of non-discrimination has enabled it to respond effectively to the needs of young people, to protect and promote their right to accurate, non-judgmental sexual and reproductive health information and services...'[28] The IPPF believes that young people 'need personal skills and confidence to practice sexual behaviour that is safe and enjoyable for them, and to negotiate the sexual relationship they want at the time that is right for them'.[29]

In 2002 the IPPF called on the United Nations to stand by its previous commitments to young people's sexual rights. Dr Pramilla Senanyake of the IPPF said: 'We believe that with the tools to make informed choices, young men and women cannot only protect themselves from the risks of HIV, unwanted pregnancy and unsafe abortion, they can also enjoy a better life with the freedom to achieve their aspirations.'[30]

The IPPF youth policy on comprehensive sex education, issued in 2006, upholds the right of young people to information that 'should enhance the independence and self-esteem of young people and provide them with the knowledge and confidence to make informed choices'.[31]

Humanism and informed choice

The British Humanist Association, in a note for the Sex Education Forum, expresses its commitment to the concept of informed choice. 'The focus of SRE should be to equip children and young people with the capacity to make informed, responsible choices about their own behaviour and activity.'[32] The Humanist Society in Scotland says that 'humanism offers a coherent and comprehensive set of moral and ethical principles and standards without recourse to religion… Humanism seeks to offer a distinct contribution to learning in all its forms, the right to make informed choices, the development of ethical and moral responsibility and the promotion of tolerance.'[33]

A statement of the American Humanist Association supports comprehensive sex education: 'We, the undersigned, declare that comprehensive sexuality education programs need to be included in all public schools as these programs are vital to the health and well being of future generations. The goal of such education is to provide facts so that students are empowered to make informed decisions regarding their sexuality.'[34]

The above statements make it clear that informed choice is a central tenet of secular humanism. The individual, without recourse to the moral law of God, is held to be capable of making his own responsible informed decisions.

A biblical critique of informed choice dogma

To understand the true nature of informed choice we need to turn to Scripture, for in the Garden of Eden we see the first invitation to mankind to make an informed choice.

At the time of creation the Lord God saw all that he had created was very good (Genesis 1:31). God placed Adam in the Garden and in his goodness had provided him with a perfect creation and an abundance of trees that were pleasant to the sight and good for food (Genesis 2:8-9). The Lord God commanded the man, 'Of every tree of the garden you may freely eat; but of the tree of the knowledge of good and evil you shall not eat, for in the day that you eat of it you shall surely die' (Genesis 2:16-17).

By giving the man a commandment, the mighty Creator was asserting his authority as the righteous Lawgiver. Man must obey God's moral law, which is holy, righteous and good (Romans 7:12). Within the constraints of God's law, man was free to choose to eat from any tree within the Garden. However, man was not free to eat of the forbidden fruit, for to do so was to rebel against God's moral law, which is lawlessness and sin. To disobey God's law results in the loss of freedom to choose for our Lord said, 'whoever commits sin is a slave of sin' (John 8:34).

The cunning serpent approached the woman and challenged the authority of God's word, 'Has God indeed said?' (Genesis 3:1). The serpent enticed Eve to disobey God's commandment by suggesting that there were no consequences for breaking God' moral law. 'You will not surely die!' (Genesis 3:4). The woman was deceived into thinking that she was free to make her own informed choice about whether or not to eat the forbidden fruit. In reality, her choice was between obeying or disobeying God's moral law, but the crafty serpent did not present it in those stark terms. The serpent asserted that if she ate of the tree not only would she not die, but she would become like God, knowing good and evil. The other information for her to take into account, in making her informed decision, was that the fruit was good for food, pleasant to the eyes and desirable for making her wise (Genesis 3:6).

Eve was deceived into believing the serpent's lie that God's commandment was optional, that it was her right to make an informed choice, and that she could do so without consequences. The reality was that her informed choice to eat the forbidden fruit flew in the face of God's commandment, and she faced the dreadful consequences of her disobedience. What this teaches us is that a *moral* decision cannot be taken without reference to the moral law of God. It also shows that moral decisions have consequences. Informed choice dogma is deceptive for it offers various sexual options without reference to God's moral law.

Our decisions with regard to sexual conduct, and every moral choice for that matter, must be made within the boundary of God's moral law. To make a choice that disregards God's law is not an informed choice but rebellion against the righteous Lawgiver. So the term 'informed choice' is really a euphemism to hide its true meaning—to hide the reality of the rebellious spirit behind a moral choice made without reference to God's word.

To advise young people that they need a large number of facts about contraception and STIs in order to make a choice about their sexual options is to suggest, as the serpent did to Eve, that God's moral law is irrelevant and can be ignored with impunity. Informed choice dogma deceives young people into believing that they are free to make a sexual choice on the basis of factual information, but such a choice is based on the wicked idea that man can decide for himself what is right and wrong.

Here then is a great biblical truth. When it comes to a moral decision, such as sexual conduct, then there is no such thing as an informed choice. The moral law of God with regard to sexual conduct is absolute—flee sexual immorality; flee also youthful lusts; abstain from the lusts of the flesh. The only choice is whether or not to obey God's moral law. It is no accident that the concept of informed choice, as revealed by the IPPF, the FPA and Brook, has come from the godless mindset of secular humanism that does not accept the moral law of God revealed in Scripture.

The presupposition of secular humanism is that we live in a universe without God and without moral absolutes. It follows that we are free to choose our own version of morality; each person is free to do whatever appears to be right in his or her own eyes. The dogma of informed choice has been devised as the means of helping autonomous man create his own system of relative morality.

Sexual options

CARE presents a young couple with this question: *To have sex or not to have sex? That is the question – discuss* (see picture page 86). Here is a clear example of informed choice dogma in practice. Both CARE and the British Humanist Association believe that sexual behaviour should be discussed in an open and objective way (see page 33) to help a young

To have sex or not to have sex?

That is the question!

evaluate

couple make an informed choice. They are given two options, to have sex or not to have sex, without reference to God's law, and invited to discuss which option most appeals to them. They are led to believe that the options are morally neutral, for they are not warned to abstain from sexual immorality (Acts 15:20). As we

have already seen, CARE's sex education helps young people develop their own values in order to answer this question.

Informed choice dogma persuades a young couple that whatever choice they make, whether it's to have sex or to abstain, it's the right choice for them. The young couple's decision depends on what they *want*, on their sexual desires, on how they feel at that moment in time, and not on any objective standard of right and wrong. All that matters, if they decide to have sex, is that they know how to practice 'safer sex' with condoms.

Why have sex?

Following the advice of the British Humanist Association that sex should be talked about openly, CARE invites young people to join a discussion group to find an answer to the question, *Why have sex?* By inviting open discussion CARE is showing that all opinions are valuable and to be respected. Having heard a variety of opinions, each young person is in a position to make an informed decision as to why they should or should not have sex. And because CARE offers no moral guidance and does not teach that sexual immorality is wrong, no opinion can be judged as wrong or immoral.

But of what value is the opinion of any young person when Scripture has spoken clearly? God's moral law as it relates to sexual conduct is not optional, or open to discussion, for 'he who commits sexual immorality sins against his own body' (1 Corinthians 6:18). It is God's will that sex should take place within the marriage union. Therefore, young people are commanded to flee sexual immorality and to abstain from the lusts of the flesh. The problem with CARE's group discussion is that it cultivates the idea that there is no moral law and therefore young people are entitled to reach their own informed answer to the question, *Why have sex?*

Discuss
Group discussion and feedback – an opportunity to express opinions
evaluate

Damnable advice

To offer young people the option of having sex without warning that promiscuity is against the moral law of God is leading them into the path of temptation. To place before young people the choice of sexual intercourse, and suggest that it is for them to make an *informed decision* on the basis of the facts, guided by their own values, is damnable advice. Those who do so should take heed of the biblical warning. Jesus said, 'Woe to the world because of enticements to sin! For enticements to sin must come, but woe to that man by whom the enticements to sin comes!' (Matthew 18:7).

This review of the concept of informed choice shows that it comes from the wisdom of man and is fundamentally opposed to biblical morality. The uncomfortable truth is that CARE's system of morality is based on the dogma of informed choice that flows from the godless worldview of secular humanism. We must conclude that CARE, a so-called Christian organisation, is indoctrinating schoolchildren into a worldly philosophy that leads them along the broad way to destruction.

(Endnotes)
1 *CARE Today*, Spring 2008, Ballet students dance to a different tune CARE's evaluate programme persuades pupils to build better relationships
2 CARE website, CARE, Get Involved, Jobs and Volunteering, evaluate Project Officer
3 Evaluate website, Turning the tide page
4 CARE's Prayer Guide, Thursday 4th January 2007 (October 2006 to January 2007)

5 Make Love Last website, values statement.

6 Love for Life website, 'Icebergs and Babies', home page

7 CareConfidential website, I'm pregnant and I don't want to be

8 CARE, *Called to Care,* A manual for Christian pregnancy crisis counselling, revised 2002, p77

9 CARE Centres Network website, Men and Crisis Pregnancy

10 Family Planning Association Manifesto for Sexual Health & Family Planning, 1990

11 Fpa website, about us, what we do

12 Brook website, Brook's mission statement, charitable objects, and values

13 Marie Stopes International website

14 Sex Education Forum, The Framework for Sex and Relationship Education, 1999, p2

15 Department of Health, *You're Welcome quality criteria: Making health services young people friendly*, 2005, DH Publications Orderline, p8

16 Review of Sex and Relationship Education (SRE) in Schools. A report by the External Steering Group (2008), item 43, item 49

17 British Pregnancy Advisory Service website, Unplanned pregnancy support and advice, Friends, What happens at the consultation appointment?

18 Planned Parenthood Alberta website, The Option of Abortion

19 Brook's website, Brook's position on abortion, Policy and research

20 Marie Stopes booklet, Abortion your questions answered

21 Family Planning Programs, Population Reports, Series J, Number 50, volume XXIX, Number 1, Spring 2001, Population Information Programme, The Johns Hopkins University Bloomberg School of Public Health, Informed Choice, Evolution of Informed Choice.

22 Ibid. Population Reports, Series J, Number 50, Evolution of Informed Choice

23 Ibid. Task Force Executive Summary, p3

24 Ibid. Task Force Executive Summary, p4

25 Ibid. Task Force Executive Summary, p5

26 POP Briefs, USAID, Centre for Population, Voluntary Participation and Informed Choice in Family Planning, usaid.gov/pdf_docs/PNACP200.pdf

27 IPPF Annual Programme Review 2002 - 2003, Young people, p61

28 Ibid. p61

29 Ibid. p62

30 IPPF website, Stand by your commitment to adolescents, IPPF urges, 1 May 2002

31 IPPF Framework for Comprehensive Sexuality Education, produced by the IPPF Adolescents Team, London, May 2006, page 2

32 Briefing note for the Sex Education Forum from the British Humanist Association, Sex and Relationships Education Review 2008.

33 Humanist Society in Scotland, The HSS leaflet on Humanism in Education, 2008

34 American Humanist Association, Free Mind, August/September 2005

9

Emergency contraception

We heard in chapter 2 that CARE's vision 'is to see the transformation of society into one that has a greater respect for the sanctity and value of human life from *fertilisation* [my italics] to its natural end'.[1] This statement obviously has great significance, for it is a declaration that CARE supports the biblical view that life starts at conception, when the ovum is fertilized by a sperm. Because God's word teaches that life starts at conception those who follow the Christian faith are opposed to emergency contraception, for its purpose is to destroy an early human embryo.

The Theology of Life

Before considering CARE's approach to emergency contraception we need to be clear about what the Bible has to say about human life. Scripture teaches that the Lord God created man in his own image. The God of Scripture is the Creator and Sustainer of all life, 'since he gives to all life, breath, and all things... for in him we live and move and have our being' (Acts 17:25, 28). The weight of Scripture points to conception, when the sperm and ovum unite, as the beginning of life. God said to Jeremiah, 'Before I formed you in the womb I knew you' (Jeremiah 1:5). An angel of the Lord said to Joseph, 'for that which is conceived in her is of the Holy Spirit' (Matthew 1:20). Boaz took Ruth, the Moabitess, and she became his wife: 'and when he went in to her, the Lord gave her conception, and she bore a son' (Ruth 4:13). They called him Obed and he was the father of Jesse, the father David. King David acknowledged that 'in sin my mother conceived me' (Psalm 51:5).

When the sperm enters the ovum a new life is created as the DNA of the man and woman join together to form the unique genetic make up of a new human being. The science of embryology shows that at conception, each normal baby obtains 46 chromosomes – 23 from each parent. Each person retains those genes for the remainder of life. Every person has his or her own genetic code, which is different from that of the mother or father. The new embryo, within hours of being created, signals his presence by producing the Early Pregnancy Factor, an immuno-suppressive protein which warns his mother's immune system not to attack him. After fertilization the new embryo is slowly sucked through the Fallopian tube and only arrives in the womb about five days after conception. During the journey through the Fallopian tube the lining of the mother's womb prepares to receive her new baby which will be implanted around day five.

John Ling, a medical biologist, in his book *The morning-after pill* (2007) explains the biblical view of conception:

> The Bible has a wonderful unity and its true meaning and teaching on any particular topic is determined, not from an isolated verse or two taken out of context, but by comparing and contrasting all of its content, concepts and themes... The outcome of examining these verses is an insistent authority and an irresistible momentum that will constrain us to conclude that the Scriptures teach: first, that human life does indeed begin at no time other than at conception and second, that all human life from day one onwards is special and precious, to be protected and cherished. In other words, the nature and status of the human embryo are clearly delineated.'[2] Ling continues, 'If you doubt that human life begins at fertilization, or if you regard the human embryo as a mere thing, then you have a fundamental argument with Scripture. Many of the major doctrines of orthodox, historic Christianity – among them, the nature of man, the foreknowledge of God, the Incarnation and our redemption – depend four-square upon these propositional truths.[3]

For those who do not accept conception as the beginning of life, there are a host of alternative views. Common is the idea that life starts at implantation, when the zygote becomes attached to the womb. Others feel that life starts when the embryo has a recognizable human shape. Another view is that life starts at viability, when the baby could survive outside the mother's womb. Some even say that life starts at birth. Yet all these views are based on arbitrary human opinion and feelings—there is nothing in Scripture to support any of these views. So the weight of Scripture, as we have seen above, is that God has decreed that life starts at conception.

The term emergency contraception is a misnomer for in most cases conception has already occurred. The purpose of emergency contraception – the so-called morning-after pill, or the intra-uterine device (IUD) – is to attack and destroy a newly created embryo, effectively a new person. As such it violates the purposes of God and breaks the Sixth Commandment; you shall not murder. Here again we see evidence of the spiritual war of the two seeds—the Seed of the woman holds to the sanctity of human life, while the seed of the serpent seeks to destroy human life (see chapter 4). Emergency contraception aims to destroy a new embryo by preventing implantation from taking place. Behind emergency contraception is an ideology that is essentially the same as that which drives the abortion industry, namely a profound disregard for the value of human life. It is an ideology that demands the pleasures of sex without consequences. It violates all that is good and holy in God's divine plan for sexual conduct.

Emergency contraception in CARE's sex quiz

As we saw in chapter 6, the *evaluate* quiz makes sure that schoolgirls and young people know the facts about emergency contraception. CARE asks:

> *After having unprotected sex a woman has 48 hours – 2 days – to get emergency contraception (the morning-after pill).*

This is a trick question, for CARE wants to emphasise the fact that emergency contraception is licensed for use for 72 hours after unprotected sex, and will have some effect beyond this time (see page 66). Moreover, CARE believes that it must inform young people that an IUD can also be used as emergency contraception. 'An IUD (coil) may be fitted up to 5 days after unprotected sex, or up to 5 days after earliest possible ovulation.' So CARE is making sure that schoolgirls don't make the mistake of thinking that they have only 2 days after 'unprotected' sex to avail themselves of emergency contraception. CARE also makes sure that young people know that 'emergency contraception may also be purchased for approximately £25 by women of 16 years old via a pharmacist'.

Emergency contraception in the UK

Before we examine CARE's policy on emergency contraception we need to understand the national context, for then we shall be in a position to assess the significance of the link from CARE's *evaluate* sex education website to their crisis pregnancy website—CareConfidential, as shown in the picture below.

In April 1982 the British Pregnancy Advisory Service (BPAS), one of the biggest providers of abortion in the UK, used a symposium at the

Royal College of Physicians to plead for the 'morning-after' pill to be made more widely available from general practitioners and family planning clinics. The first hormonal emergency contraceptive product was approved in the UK in January 1984 and marketed in October of the same year. The BPAS pointed to the need for a well-publicised nationwide 'morning-after' service within the NHS and is proud of being the first organisation in the UK to offer a routine service for the 'after sex' contraceptive pill, and continues to encourage health care professionals to provide this pill to a woman before she needs to use it.

The family planning lobby, despite its propaganda that condoms provide all-in-one protection against pregnancy and STIs, was aware that contraception on its own could not lower teenage pregnancy numbers—it needed to be backed up by emergency contraception and abortion. So it is no surprise that the Government sees emergency contraception as a useful weapon in its struggle against unwanted teenage pregnancies. Sex education guidance, issued to all schools and health authorities in 2000, explains that teaching schoolchildren about contraception *and* emergency contraception is at the heart of the Government's strategy to reduce teenage pregnancy. Trained staff in secondary schools are required to give full information about different types of contraception, including emergency contraception.[4]

Over the counter emergency contraception

In February 2000 a report from the parliamentary All Party Pharmacy Group recommended that emergency hormonal contraception should be available from community pharmacies without the need for prescription. The British Medical Association strongly endorsed the recommendation, 'We believe that supplies should be available at no cost to the patient in the same way that post-coital contraception already is available free of charge from GPs.'[5]

In January 2001 a change in the law allowed the sale of emergency contraception over the counter to girls aged over 16. The measure was formally ordered by the Health Secretary Alan Milburn and enthusiastically welcomed by the FPA and BPAS.

In the two years after emergency contraception became available without a doctor's prescription, the number of women obtaining emergency contraception from chemists, walk-in centres and minor injury units almost doubled. A spokeswoman for BPAS said: 'The decision to allow women to buy emergency contraception from chemists was a tremendous step forward and has evidently been successful. The next logical step would be to allow women to buy emergency contraception in advance of need from their local pharmacy.' And a spokeswoman for the FPA added: 'The FPA has long been campaigning for better access to emergency contraception so we are pleased that more women are finding it easier to get hold of it through a variety of different outlets.'[6]

Over the last two decades emergency contraception has been energetically promoted by the sex education industry as a means of preventing unwanted pregnancies. This policy has been so successful that by the mid-1990s almost 800 thousand prescriptions per year were issued to women in England and Wales, which was more than the total annual number of births. In the financial year 2004/5 community contraception clinics issued 24.5 thousand prescriptions for emergency contraception to girls under 16, and 72 thousand to young women aged 16 to 19.[7] The number obtaining over the counter emergency contraception from pharmacies is not known. Yet the Government now has a major campaign to increase the use of emergency contraception among teenagers.

International Consortium for Emergency Contraception

The driving force behind the worldwide growth of emergency contraception is the International Planned Parenthood Federation (IPPF). It has long recognised the potential of emergency contraception in controlling population growth. In November 1981 the IPPF endorsed the use of what it chose to call post-coital contraception after 'unprotected' intercourse.

In 1995 the Rockefeller Foundation convened a high level meeting to discuss ideas for increasing the use of emergency contraception. After the meeting a group of seven international organisations set up the International Consortium for Emergency Contraception to promote emergency contraception as a method for reducing unintended pregnancies worldwide. Among the founding organisations were the IPPF, the World Health Organisation (WHO) and the Population Council. The International Consortium has actively encouraged interest in emergency contraception through meetings with public sector agencies and non-governmental organisations and set out to demonstrate that emergency contraception has an important role to play in preventing unwanted pregnancies.

CARE promotes emergency contraception

Having outlined the massive growth of emergency contraception in the UK over the last two decades, and the role played by the British Pregnancy Advisory Service and the IPPF, we can now turn again to CARE. What we find is that CARE is using its network of Christian crisis pregnancy counselling centres, many of which are attached to evangelical churches, to promote the use of emergency contraception.

A schoolgirl who visits CARE's *evaluate* website, concerned because she has had 'unprotected' sex, is provided with a hyperlink to the CareConfidential website, where she is advised to have a pregnancy test and given advice on emergency contraception. Once the schoolgirl knows the outcome of her pregnancy test she is reassured that:

> The trained advisor will help you, when you are ready, to look at your situation, your feelings and the options that are open to you. If your result was negative, you may still need to talk to someone about any of the following: If you have had unprotected sex within the last 72 hours and want to find out about emergency contraception, click here.

CARE's commitment to the dogma of informed choice means that a schoolgirl must be given all the information she needs to help her decide whether or not she wants to use emergency contraception. The fact that conception has probably already taken place is of no concern to CARE. The CareConfidential website provides information on the methods of emergency contraception that are available, namely progestogen-only pills and the Copper IUD, which is inserted into the womb. According to CareConfidential both of these methods can be very effective but within a certain time limit.[7] Having gained an understanding of how emergency contraception works a schoolgirl must decide whether or not she wants to use it. The CareConfidential website helps her to make an informed decision—the italics are mine:

CareConfidential
For pregnancy and
post-abortion support

SEARCH SITE

0800 028 2228

Online Advisor
Secure Confidential Personal

› Home   › Find Centre   › About Us   › Contact Us

Your Questions Answered

I might be pregnant
I am pregnant
My partner is pregnant
My daughter is pregnant
What about having a baby?
What about adoption?
What about abortion?
I had an abortion
Emergency contraception

Six Ways to Find Help

Local Centres
Helpline
Online Advisor
Your Questions Answered
Peoples Stories
Services Search

CareConfidential

About Us

Emergency contraception

Emergency contraception is a method of preventing pregnancy after unprotected sex or if your other contraception has failed. It is **not** 100% effective. Pregnancy can still occur.

There are two methods of emergency contraception:

- Progestogen-only pills
- Copper IUD (intra-uterine device) inserted into the womb.

Both of these methods can be very effective but within a certain time limit.

How do they work?

Progestogen-only pills:

- Prevent ovulation if it has not already occurred
- Prevent implantation of an egg that has already been fertilised.

The IUD:

- Helps to prevent fertilisation early in the menstrual cycle by hindering sperm from reaching the egg.
- Makes it harder for a fertilised egg to implant in the womb.

Is it for me?

- You may be feeling that your situation is quite urgent, but it is also important to consider how progestogen-only pills work. Depending on the time in your menstrual cycle that you take the pills, it works in different ways.

- Taken before you ovulate (release an egg) it prevents the egg being released. Taken after you ovulate, it may prevent an already ferti-lised egg from implanting (settling into the womb). *Conception will already have taken place.*

- If you are taking any other medication, you will need to consult a doctor before taking emergency contraception pills

The IUD does not prevent an egg being released. It can prevent an egg from being fertilised, but it can also prevent a fertilised egg from implanting. Again, this means that *conception has already taken place.*

It is important that you consider carefully what this means, because you may want to think about when life begins. To understand this better, you may find it *helpful to look at the* [BBC] *Pregnancy Timeline.* [Click Here]

The above advice is available to schoolgirls who have entered the CareConfidential website through the hyperlink provided by the *evaluate* website. Clearly, one of the aims of CARE's sex education project is to help schoolgirls and young women gain access to emergency contracep-tion and abortion. Those with moral concerns about using emergency contraception are referred to the BBC timeline.

CARE's hypocrisy

At the start of this chapter we saw CARE's claim that their vision 'is to see the transformation of society into one that has a greater respect for the sanctity and value of human life from *fertilisation* [my italics] to its natural end'. In his July 2009 newsletter Lyndon Bowring writes in bold letters, 'We will not give up on defending the sanctity of human life'. This is the message to those Christians who provide financial support. But CARE's assertion that it supports the sanctity of human life is a false statement, for by its promotion of emergency contraception CARE is quite prepared to destroy a newly conceived human embryo. So CARE does not respect the sanctity of human life from fertilization—CARE is deceiving its supporters.

CARE's policy on emergency contraception is similar to that of the IPPF, the FPA and the BPAS. Let us be absolutely clear on this point— CARE does not oppose the use of emergency contraception. Indeed, while acknowledging that conception may have taken place, CARE promotes emergency contraception as a useful method for dealing with the concern caused by 'unprotected' sex. And to help a young woman who may have doubts as to when life begins, CARE refers her to the pregnancy timeline prepared by the BBC, despite the fact that the BBC is steeped in secular humanism. So it is no surprise that the BBC's timeline refers to a new embryo as a ball of multiplying cells and gives no guidance as to when life begins. This means that a schoolgirl or young woman, having viewed the BBC pictures, must decide for herself when she thinks life begins.

But why does CARE, which claims to be a Christian organisation, not refer a young woman to the Scriptures? Is the God of Scripture, the Creator and Sustainer of life, the One in whom we live and move and have our being, unable to answer her doubts? The unfortunate young woman is given no spiritual guidance by CARE to help her respect the sanctity and value of human life. She is given no guidance to help her understand the consequences of her actions. As with condoms, so with emergency contraception, CARE ignores biblical truth. As with condoms, so with emergency contraception, CARE's advice is without moral guidance. This is a very serious matter, for CARE is using its sex education project to promote emergency contraception among schoolchildren and young people, and is doing so in the name of the Christian faith.

(Endnotes)

1 CARE's website, Vision, http://www.care.org.uk/Group/Group.aspx?id=10608
2 John Ling, *The morning-after pill*, The Christian Institute, 2007, p50
3 Ibid. page 54
4 *Sex and Relationship Education Guidance*, DfEE, July 2000, p10

5 News release from BMA, issued on Monday 28 February 2000
6 BBC news 24, 'Morning after pill access widens', Wednesday, 29 September 2004, UK
7 NHS Contraceptives Services, England: 2004 - 05
8 www.careconfidential.com/EmergencyContraception.aspx

10

Self-esteem

We have heard that the *evaluate* project works 'from the understanding that many issues confronting young people stem from *low self-esteem*'.[1] At the heart of CARE's sex education programme 'is the premise that each person is a unique and valuable individual. *Evaluate* encourages the development of self-worth and seeks to cultivate a healthy respect for self and others.'[2] CARE's sex education policy aims to 'develop personal and social skills including negotiation, assertiveness, self-esteem'.[3]

The Northern Ireland sex education programme, Love for Life, is a classic example of a programme based on an appeal to self-esteem. It invites young people to make 'informed and mature sexual health choices' on the basis of information and positive self-esteem.[4] And 'self-esteem is when you feel good about yourself, and you feel confident that there are things you can do and do well. If you feel good about yourself, you have positive or high self-esteem. But if you feel bad about yourself, you have negative or low self-esteem... Successful people know that to meet their goals, they have to feel good about themselves. Being successful means doing your best, learning from your mistakes and feeling good about yourself – that will make you a winner!'[5]

Sex education promotes positive self-esteem

The Government's sex education strategy promotes self-esteem as a psychological tool that can help children make healthy sexual choices. 'Personal development should be a key element of teenage programmes as confidence and positive self-esteem will determine decisions made by

young people.'[6] Guidance from the Department for Education emphasises the importance of building self-esteem in children and young
people in both primary and secondary schools.[7] Sex education 'enables
young people to mature, to build up their confidence and self-esteem and
understand the reasons for delaying sexual activity'.[8]

The Government's Teenage Parenthood Working Group claimed
that the reason young people make unhealthy sexual choices is because
they have low self-esteem. 'Young people with positive self-esteem are
much less likely to become teenage parents. Efforts to reduce teenage
parenthood rates in both the short and long-term must focus on improving self-esteem among young people.'[9] The national strategy to reduce
teenage pregnancies says that, 'Personal development should be a key
element of teenage programmes as confidence and positive self-esteem
will determine decisions made by young people.'[10]

A report of the Teenage Pregnancy Unit tells of a project with young
women who had low self-esteem and very little knowledge of sexual
health. The aim of the project was to increase their self-esteem and sexual
knowledge. One young woman who was under pressure from her boyfriend to have sex said that the project gave her the confidence to make
the right decision for herself.[11]

The FPA policy statement on Sex and Relationship Education (SRE)
emphasises the importance of self-esteem. 'SRE must be inclusive and
relevant and should meet the educational and emotional needs of all
pupils. An emphasis on qualities within relationships such as respect,
honesty, trust, and self-esteem avoids the stigmatization or promotion of
any one form of relationship or sexual orientation.'[12] Brook believes that
'positive self-esteem and strong emotional and social skills are essential
in enabling young people to manage and enjoy their relationships and
sexual health'.[13] Many sex education manuals contain activities to help
children develop positive self-esteem.

The WHO believes that self-esteem dogma should be part of sex
education. 'In general, self-esteem means that the teenager should feel
good about himself or herself, have self-confidence and have the ability
to make the right decisions. Self-esteem also means being able to com-
municate clearly with other people and have self-respect. An adolescent

with such self-esteem is more likely to avoid STIs by delaying sex, having only one partner, and using condoms regularly.'[14]

Planned Parenthood promotes self-esteem as part of its sex education agenda for parents. 'Children of all ages need to feel loved and valued. When parents or guardians take time to remind them how special they are, it bolsters their self-esteem. The link between self-esteem and adolescent sexual behaviour has received much attention. Healthy self-esteem increases the likelihood of healthy, more responsible choices – about sex as well as other issues. A young child's self-esteem requires conscious tending and nurturing. Parents are just right for the job.'[15]

The roots of self-esteem dogma

Self-esteem dogma has its roots in the teachings of the humanist psychologists Abraham Maslow and Carl Rogers, both of whom were given the honour of being American Humanist of the Year. In *A Theory of Human Motivation* Maslow emphasised the human need for self-esteem. He claimed that all people have a need for a stable, firmly based, high evaluation of themselves. 'Satisfaction of the self-esteem need leads to feelings of self-confidence, worth, strength, capability and adequacy of being useful and necessary in the world. But thwarting of these needs produces feelings of inferiority, of weakness and of helplessness. These feelings in turn give rise to either basic discouragement or else compensatory or neurotic trends.'[16]

The ideas of Carl Rogers have also had a large impact on the self-esteem movement. He believed that as human nature is basically good, human beings should feel good about themselves, and accept themselves as they are. According to Rogers, human beings value positive self-regard, self-esteem, self-worth and a positive self-image. Lack of self-esteem hinders psychological growth and prevents people from developing to their full potential.

It is not difficult to see that self-esteem dogma comes from the ideas of humanistic psychologists who believe in the inherent goodness of human nature and reject the concept of sin. To find a plausible explanation for the problem of human misery and unhappiness they have developed the psychological construct of 'low self-esteem' in an attempt to explain away the effects of sin on the human condition. In *Unmasking the New Age* (1986) Douglas Groothuis points out that 'in humanistic psychology the self is seen as the radiant heart of health, and psychotherapy must strive to get the person in touch with that source of goodness... This is the message at the core of New Age teaching.'[17]

A massive self-esteem industry has invaded virtually every aspect of life, including the arenas of education, health, religion and commerce. We are continually warned of the scourge of low self-esteem that threatens all people and causes a catalogue of social problems, including teenage pregnancies.

The problems with self-esteem dogma

Kathryn Ecclestone, professor of education at Oxford Brookes University, points out that 'a lack of robust research does not stop the Department for Education and Skills making sweeping assertions about links between poor emotional literacy, crime, marriage breakdown, offending, anti-social behaviour, disruption in schools and mental health. These are translated into official targets and guidance for "social, emotional and affective learning" in primary schools, soon to be extended into secondary schools.'[18] A deluge of guidance is directed at teaching schoolchildren the skills of emotional literacy. In many primary schools a therapeutic ritual encourages children to talk about their feelings, and helps them to feel good about themselves and hopes to improve their self-esteem.

The problem with the appeal to self-esteem as a guide to decision making is that it ignores the moral dimension of life. The psychological approach claims that those with positive self-esteem are empowered to make 'healthy' sexual choices, while those with poor self-esteem are likely to make 'unhealthy' choices. At the heart of the self-esteem approach is the idea that there is no right or wrong, only 'healthy' and 'unhealthy' choices. So promiscuity is not wrong, but may be an 'unhealthy' choice. The appeal to self-esteem persuades young people that their sexual choices can be made on the basis of how they feel about themselves and not on any objective moral standard. The Love for Life programme reassures young people of 'the value and worth of each person' and informs them that they are 'special no matter what choices they make in any area of their lives'.[19] In other words, self-esteem is all about feeling good regardless of how I behave, and getting what I want, with no moral compass.

Another major problem with self-esteem dogma is the focus on self. The Christian faith is about self-control and self-denial. The idea that we should look within ourselves for empowerment to make positive choices is to deny the doctrine of original sin, to deny the truth that the human heart is deceitful above all things, and desperately wicked (Jeremiah 17:9). The idea that high self-esteem will help young people overcome the lusts of the flesh is contrary to Scripture. The Bible teaches that a moral choice comes from obeying God's law. 'How can a young man cleanse his way? By taking heed according to your word. With my whole heart I have sought you; oh let me not wander from your commandments! Your word have I hidden in my heart that I might not sin against you' (Psalm 119:9-11). Self-esteem dogma, on the other hand, teaches that a 'positive' choice is generated by my subjective emotions—that which makes me feel good is a 'positive' choice.

CARE and self-esteem

CARE's promotion of self-esteem dogma among schoolchildren is another example of its deep commitment to the ways and thinking of the world. CARE is simply following the Government's agenda, and the example of secular sex educators such as the FPA and Brook. CARE could teach about sexual conduct from Scripture, but it has chosen to follow the theories that come from the humanistic school of psychology. Why does CARE do this? Because it conforms to the thinking and pattern of the world. 'They have perverted their way; they have forgotten the Lord their God' (Jeremiah 3:21).

(Endnotes)

1 Evaluate website. Journalists, turning the tide
2 Evaluate website. Page Sex or no sex, that is the question?
3 Evaluate website. Page Evaluate education policy
4 Cited from, Love for Life website, www.loveforlife.org.uk
5 Cited from, Who's choosing, www.careincrisis.org.uk
6 Teenage Pregnancy and Parenthood Strategy and Action Plan 2002 - 2007, Department of

Health, Social Services and Public Safety, November 2002
7 Ibid. Sex and Relationship Education Guidance, DfEE, p9,10
8 Ibid. p4
9 Myths & Reality: Teenage Pregnancy and Parenthood, Report of the Teenage Parenthood Working Group, November 2000
10 Teenage Pregnancy and Parenthood Strategy and Action Plan 2002 - 2007, Department of Health, Social Services and Public Safety, November 2002, p12
11 Teenage pregnancy next steps; Guidance for Local Authorities and Primary Care Trusts on Effective Delivery of Local Strategies, Department for Education and Skills, 2006, p36
12 FPA policy statement on Sex and Relationship Education, May 2009
13 Brook training 2009 brochure, A rights based approach to sexual health work with young people, p9
14 WHO/WPRO, Sexually transmitted infections: Briefing kit for teachers (2001), p5
15 Planned Parenthood of SW Oregon, 2007, There's no place like home for sex education
16 Abraham Maslow, *A Theory of Human Motivation*, p383
17 Douglas Groothuis, *Unmasking the New Age*, Intervarsity Press, 1986, p78
18 *The Guardian*, 27 February 2007, Kathryn Ecclestone, All in the mind
19 Cited from, Love for Life website, www.loveforlife.org.uk

11

CARE's descent into apostasy

So what is going on in Christian sex education? In this book we have lifted the veil and looked in some detail at CARE's sex education programme. We have seen that it teaches about sex in a way that ignores God's moral law and trivializes sexual immorality. We have seen that it supplies children and young people with a great deal of information about contraception – especially how to use and dispose of condoms – and that it invites them to make an informed choice whether or not to have sex. We have seen that it helps children overcome their feelings of low self-esteem.

CARE's non-directive abortion counselling

Yet our examination of CARE's sex education programme would be incomplete without making reference to their network of crisis pregnancy counselling centres. CareConfidential is a national freephone helpline, which offers counselling to anyone whatever their age, beliefs, background or circumstance. According to CARE the mission of its pregnancy counselling 'is to declare Christian truth and demonstrate Christ's compassion in society'.[1]

Making a decision

The leaflet *Making a Decision* provides an example of the type of counselling that is offered by CARE. The purpose of the leaflet, available from CareConfidential, is to help a woman decide what she should do with her unwanted pregnancy. 'Sometimes it's hard to make choices because choices always involve both gains and losses. With each of the options open to you – keeping the baby, adoption or abortion – there are gains and losses. You could think about what you would gain with each of the options and write them down. Then you could also write down what you feel you would lose with each of the options. These may include practical things like money, time, freedom, job and the baby itself, but also other things like self-respect, feeling at peace with yourself or feeling secure.'[2]

Having made her list of the pros and cons of each option, including abortion, the woman must decide which option is best for her. She is encouraged to consult her deeper feelings and beliefs. 'Think about the three options. Are any of them instinctively right or wrong to you?'

So in order to make her decision she must consider the gains and loses in economic and psychological terms and consult her instinctive feelings. There is no moral guidance and the woman is not told that abortion is wrong. Indeed, the three options are treated as moral equivalents. CARE has effectively demoralised abortion.

In my book, *What is going on in Christian Crisis Pregnancy Counselling?* (2005) I examine the advice that comes from a number of CARE's counselling centres:

> What is so sad is that desperate women who turn to a Christian organisation in their hour of need are given advice that is based on the spirit of the age. What all these examples have in common is that they are devoid of moral guidance. God's law is simply ignored as irrelevant. It is as if the Bible, which contains wisdom from above, does not exist. Rather than explain why abortion is wrong, women are encouraged to make a pragmatic choice based on their feelings.[3]

Nearly 200 delegates at the CARE Centres Network national conference were made aware of the contradiction between non-directive counselling and the message of the Bible. They were told by chairman Dr Phil Clarke that 'walking in grace and truth can often seem difficult. If we concentrate *too much on truth* we may become legalistic – if we err *too far on the side of grace* [my italics], we may wander into licence.'[4] The head of CARE's counselling network, Joanna Thompson responded, 'It was a message about the balance between truth and grace which encouraged and affirmed the volunteers.'[5]

CARE's spurious conflict between truth and grace comes from the reluctance of its counsellors to tell women that abortion is wrong. CARE rationalizes its position by inferring that to tell a woman that abortion is wrong is 'too much truth' and legalistic. However, it is sensitive to the criticism that non-directive counselling errs on the side of 'too much grace' that leads to licence and condones abortion. This means that CARE's counsellors have the impossible task of finding the correct balance between truth and grace. So how do CARE's counsellors deal with this dilemma? By ignoring God's moral law—non-directive counsellors simply give an impartial view of the advantages and disadvantages of each option and help a woman to decide for herself what she thinks is the right thing to do with her pregnancy.

So the real objective of CARE's counselling is to help a woman make the choice that is right for her. CARE's approach, which describes the pros and cons of abortion, is based on the philosophy of moral relativism. In CARE's view there are no moral absolutes, and God's moral law is replaced by situation ethics. Is CARE being faithful to its stated mission *to declare Christian truth*? Certainly not! CARE's abortion counselling stands opposed to God's truth, which alone declares right and wrong. 'I the Lord, speak the truth; I declare what is right' (Isaiah 45:19).

In my book on Christian pregnancy counselling I compare CARE's model with that of the pro-choice British Pregnancy Advisory Service (BPAS). My conclusion is that the non-directive, non-judgemental counselling provided by CARE exhibits all the essential characteristics of the pro-choice abortion counselling movement.[6] Here is what I wrote:

> It does not take much insight to see that CARE's pro-choice ideology, which encourages a woman to do as she wants with her pregnancy, is perfectly consistent with the pagan ethic. By offering a pregnant woman the option of abortion CARE has legitimised lawlessness. By giving a pregnant woman non-judgemental advice regarding her pregnancy, CARE is following the doctrine of moral relativism. By persuading a woman that her feelings are a guide to what she should do about her pregnancy, CARE is rejecting the word of the Lord. Taken as a whole, CARE's ideology is amoral and CARE is an apostate organisation.[7]

107

How do we understand CARE's descent into apostasy? As with most heresies, it starts with a rejection of the authority of Scripture, which opens the way for all kinds of other false teaching. Those who reject the authority of Scripture also deny the absolutes of God's moral law and fall into lawlessness and immorality.

CARE's source of moral authority

Evangelical Christians believe that Scripture carries the full authority of God. 'No prophecy of Scripture is of any private interpretation, for prophecy never came by the will of man, but holy men of God spoke as they were moved by the Holy Spirit' (2 Peter 1:20-21). Scripture is the only infallible authority for the Christian faith, and contains all knowledge necessary for salvation and a life of holiness. So the Christian life is defined by the authority of Scripture. This means that both Christian doctrine and Christian conduct are to be governed by Scripture.

The divine plan for sexual conduct, outlined in chapter 4, is based on the authority of Scripture and demonstrates the wisdom and character of God. It declares God's will for sexual conduct, and is the rule of life for the Christian. It is the only sure and true guide to sexual conduct and what the Christian Church should teach to men, women and children. The difference between the divine plan for sexual conduct and CARE's model of sex education is like the difference between day and night.

CARE, having chosen to ignore the authority of Scripture, has turned

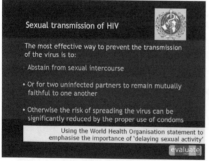

Using the World Health Organisation statement to emphasise the importance of 'delaying sexual activity'

to the authority of the World Health Organisation (WHO) to formulate its approach to sexual conduct. In accordance with the WHO position, CARE's policy on condoms, discussed on page 57, states: 'Safer sex includes non-penetrative sex and sex using condoms'.

CARE's advice on preventing STIs is based on guidance from the WHO, as shown in the picture. CARE's leaflet, *Quite a Catch*, discussed on page 18, tells young people that 'The World Health Organisation has stated that the best way to avoid becoming infected with an STI is to stay faithful to an uninfected partner for life.'

CARE is a keen exponent of the ABC approach to sex education. The *evaluate* website has this message for young people: 'There's an easy answer to the fear of getting sexually transmitted infections. We can choose to be safe, but how?' And here is CARE's answer: 'It's as easy as ABC...'[8] And CARE justifies its ABC approach by referring to the WHO, as shown in the picture. Marie Stopes International is also a keen exponent of the ABC approach. Indeed, an examination of the picture on page 6 will show that CARE and Marie Stopes teach the same ABC model of sex education.

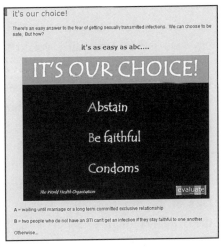

So CARE's sex education programme is built on the policies of the WHO, an agency of the United Nations, and not on Scripture. Here we should note that the first Director General of the WHO, Dr Brock Chisholm, was Humanist of the Year in 1959. There can be no doubt that WHO policies on sexual health mirror the aims and objectives of secular humanism. The reason CARE follows the WHO so closely is because the two organisations share a commitment to the agenda of human rights and the worldview of secular humanism. 'Can two walk together unless they are agreed?' (Amos 3:3).

CARE's sex education is amoral

The main objection to CARE's sex education is that it teaches about sexual conduct without reference to God's moral law. CARE openly admits that its purpose is to provide a secure environment in which schoolchildren can 'develop their own values and acquire the life skills necessary to make and carry out healthy decisions'.[9] So rather than teach biblical standards, CARE helps schoolchildren *develop their own values*. CARE does not recognise the concept of sexual immorality and does not use the word. Its non-judgemental approach does not describe any type of sexual activity as wrong or perverted and it does not warn young people of the consequences of sexual immorality. CARE's commitment to informed choice dogma encourages young people to make decisions about their sexual behaviour on the basis of the 'facts' about condoms and STIs and what they feel to be right in their own eyes. In a word, CARE's approach to sex education is amoral.

Ungodly associations

Scripture is clear that Christians should not join themselves to unbelievers. 'Do not be unequally yoked together with unbelievers. For what fellowship has righteousness with lawlessness? And what communion has light with darkness? And what accord has Christ with Belial? Or what part has a believer with an unbeliever? (2 Corinthians 6:14-15). The psalmist says, 'Blessed is the man who walks not in the counsel of the ungodly, nor stands in the path of sinners, nor sits in the seat of the scornful; but his delight is in the law of the Lord' (Psalm 1:1-2).

CARE has asked its supporters to pray that God will give members of the Sex Education Forum, which include the FPA and Brook, the British Humanist Association; Stonewall; Friends and Family of Gay, Lesbian and Bisexuals; Terrence Higgins Trust and the Lesbian and Gay Christian Movement, among others, wisdom to help young people live fulfilled and healthy lives. CARE's prayer guide offers this prayer (26th September 2007):

> Father, we pray for the members of the national Sex Education Forum and all those responsible for the policies, curriculum and teaching of SRE. Please grant them wisdom to see how children and young people can be helped to live fulfilled and healthy lives without engaging in inappropriate activities and relationships. Amen.

CARE must be aware that the national Sex Education Forum is in the forefront of the revolution against biblical standards of sexual conduct in this country. The Forum has been promoting links between schools and sexual health services for several years. As a consequence an increasing number of secondary schools are providing on site contraceptive services for their pupils.

The Forum's Sex Education Charter for children and young people, published in 2008, was written by young people who used material from Somerset 2BU Youth Group—a lesbian, gay, bisexual and transsexual organisation. According to the Charter, children and young people want more sex education and want to be safe and healthy.

The Charter says that 'to stay safe we [children and young people] need to learn the facts about contraception and know where we can get them from, with opportunities to take part in practical demonstrations'. And 'to be healthy we need to learn when we are ready for sex, and how to make decisions without being influenced or pressurised by anybody or any external forces'. The Forum is promoting the idea that children should make their sexual decisions without being influenced by the moral guidance that comes from their parents and the church.

According to the Charter, to be healthy children and young people also need to learn 'about a diverse range of relationships and how they are *all natural and normal* [my italics], and how to have safe sex'.[10] The Forum wants children to learn about a diverse range of relationships, and that obviously includes same-sex relationships. In the eyes of the Forum, no form or type of sexual behaviour is wrong or perverted and there is no such thing as sexual immorality.

CARE's prayer is that God will give wisdom to the Forum and its members 'to see how children and young people can be helped to live fulfilled and healthy lives without engaging in inappropriate activities'. So CARE believes that the Forum and its members are able to help children live fulfilled and healthy lives. And what are the 'inappropriate activities' that are of concern to CARE? As far as the Forum is concerned the only 'inappropriate activity' is for children to have sex without condoms.

What are we to make of this prayer? Christ said 'woe to that man by whom offenses come' (Matthew 18:7). Scripture warns, 'have no fellowship with the unfruitful works of darkness, but rather expose them' (Ephesians 5:11). But CARE is asking its supporters to pray for those who cause children to fall into sin. In reality, CARE is not only sitting in the seat of the scornful, but is asking its members to pray for the counsel of the ungodly.

We have seen CARE quote comments from Terrence Higgins Trust

and Brook (pages 74-75) in support of the claim that children are in desperate need of more sex education. We have also seen CARE use the
salacious teenage magazines *Just 17* (page 15) and *Bliss* (page 76) to
support its sex education agenda. Scripture warns, 'Do not put your hand
with the wicked to be an unrighteous witness. You shall not follow a
crowd to do evil' (Exodus 23:1-2).

CARE, condoms and emergency contraception

As a consequence of CARE's moral bankruptcy and its association with
the counsel of the ungodly, it teaches about condoms and emergency
contraception in the same way that they do. Indeed, CARE's cartoon of
a smiling condom (see picture) reveals its commitment to the condom

culture of the sex education industry.

Advising children that, *It's OK
to use KY jelly with condoms to aid
lubrication,* places CARE firmly in
the camp of Brook and Marie Stopes.
And CARE promotes emergency
contraception among schoolgirls
who visit their CareConfidential
website in the full knowledge that
emergency contraception destroys an early human embryo. And because
CARE no longer accepts the authority of Scripture it refers young people
to the BBC for moral guidance.

We have seen enough to understand CARE's real motivation. For more
than a decade CARE has been involved in the sex education industry,
promoting itself as the Christian voice in matters of sexual conduct. It has
received a great deal of support from churches and few have questioned
its approach. In *Lessons in Depravity* I documented CARE's approach
and warned of the danger of following CARE's sex education agenda:

> So we must ask the question: In what way does CARE's version of sex
> education differ from that of the secular sex educators? CARE, like the
> FPA and Brook, believes that primary schoolchildren should be taught a
> sexual vocabulary. CARE, like the FPA and Brook, believes that parents

should be encouraged to talk to their children about sex. CARE, like the FPA and Brook, believes that children should be taught the facts about sexual intercourse, STDs, abortion and contraception. CARE, like the FPA and Brook, believes that dedicated family planning clinics which give young people advice on how to use contraception, can be effective. CARE, like Brook and the FPA, has used the teenage magazine *Just 17* to promote its sex education messages…

One of the most concerning aspects of CARE's approach to sex education is its moral relativism—in CARE's version of sex education there are no moral absolutes… Indeed, CARE is promoting an amoral ideology that is indistinguishable from that of the FPA and Brook. CARE makes no attempt to teach young people about God's standard of sexual purity, or the Christian virtues of modesty, chivalry, chastity and fidelity.[11]

CARE's response to *Lessons in Depravity* was simply to ignore the criticism. No attempt has been made to answer the serious charges against them. And such is the lethargy within the church when it comes to moral issues that most Christian leaders have chosen not to become involved in what they regard as a controversial matter. In the succeeding five years CARE has developed the *evaluate* programme, which is now widely accepted as a 'Christian' version of sex education.

CARE takes on the mantle of Balaam

CARE's sex education programme stands condemned by Scripture. Jude, the servant of Christ, warns the church to be on its guard against false teachers who slip secretly into the fellowship and turn the grace of God into sexual immorality. 'For certain men have crept in unnoticed, who long ago were marked out for this condemnation, ungodly men, who turn the grace of our God into lewdness and deny the only Lord God and our Lord Jesus Christ' (Jude 4). Surely this Scripture applies to the ministry of CARE, an organisation that is turning the grace of God into a licence for immorality.

The accusation against CARE is that it has taken on the mantle of Balaam, the mad prophet who loved the wages of unrighteousness and enticed God's people into sexual immorality with the women of Moab. CARE, like Balaam, has the appearance of being on God's side, but its heart is devoted to the amoral ideology of the sex education industry. It teaches about sexual behaviour in a way that encourages sexual immorality, claiming that such teaching is consistent with the Christian message. But CARE's teaching is based on the authority of the WHO and not on God's word. The only conclusion we can reach is that CARE is a false organisation that is bringing the gospel of Christ into disrepute.

We have seen the stark difference between CARE's so-called 'Christian' version of sex education and the divine plan of sexual conduct. And so we must ask the question – on whose side is CARE in the perpetual spiritual war between the seed of the serpent and the Seed of the woman? The answer is obvious for CARE has chosen to join with the sexual revolutionaries and profane the name of God.

The great evangelical compromise

This book has been written as a record of CARE's amoral ministry among children and young people. It is also a warning to the church to be on its guard against false teaching. The apostle Paul said that 'savage wolves will come in among you, not sparing the flock' (Acts 20:29). Our Lord gave this warning to his disciples. 'Beware of false prophets, who come to you in sheep's clothing, but inwardly they are ravenous wolves. You will know them by their fruits. Do men gather grapes from thornbushes or figs from thistles? Even so, every good tree bears good fruit, but a bad tree bears bad fruit. A good tree cannot bear bad fruit, nor can a bad tree bear good fruit. Every tree that does not bear good fruit is cut down and thrown into the fire. Therefore by their fruits you will know them' (Matthew 7:15-20).

A good tree does not teach children to develop their *own values* with regard to sexual conduct. A good tree does not show children a cartoon picture of a smiling condom. A good tree does not teach children about emergency contraception and KY jelly for lubrication. A good tree does not tell children that an easy answer to the fear of STI's is the ABC menu of sexual options. A good tree does not use the sex survey of *Bliss* magazine as a justification for its sex education programme. On the contrary, a good tree teaches children to obey God's moral law. A good tree teaches children and young people the divine plan of sexual conduct from the

Scriptures, and emphasises the virtues of chastity, modesty, and self-control as outlined in chapter 4.

CARE's outrageous journey into sexual immorality is surely symptomatic of a far deeper malaise within evangelical Christianity in the UK. The great shame is that CARE has been able to teach its false, amoral dogma for over a decade from within the heart of the Christian faith, and there has been hardly a voice raised in opposition. Indeed, the evangelical church has not only remained silent, it continues to support CARE's amoral sexual philosophy. Those who support CARE need to understand that they are vicariously responsible for *evaluate... informing choice.* They will be called to give an account on that Day.

A large part of the problem is that many in the evangelical churches no longer take sin seriously. Few in the evangelical churches are outraged that children are being systematically indoctrinated into amorality by the sex education industry; few lament that the lives of children are being ruined by the promotion of sexual immorality; few are prepared to oppose wickedness and take an uncompromising stand for righteousness. The church, in its comfortable gospel, is careful not to cause offence. The old-fashioned biblical virtues have long ago been forgotten, and are no longer taught. Indeed, it is considered to be embarrassing even to mention the word chastity and modern evangelical Christians do not recognise, let alone teach, that modesty and self-control are essential Christian virtues.

Inevitable judgement

Scripture teaches that following Israel's sexual sin with the women of Moab, Israel yoked itself to the Baal of Peor and the anger of the Lord was kindled, and 24 thousand people died in the plague of God's judgement (Numbers 25). Scripture makes it clear the God held the leaders of Israel accountable for the moral collapse. The apostle Paul quotes this story as an example and warning that the Church of Christ should not tolerate sexual immorality in its midst. It is important for those in positions of leadership, that is pastors and elders, to understand that God holds them responsible for allowing CARE to bring its sexual immorality into the church.

Today CARE has yoked itself to the sexual immorality of the World Health Organisation, the Sex Education Forum, the FPA, Brook and the British Government. Rather than teach the divine plan for sexual conduct, CARE has chosen to lead children into sexual immorality. The Lord's anger is being aroused and judgement is inevitable and dreadful. Those who think that this is a small matter do not understand the holiness of God. A sceptre of righteousness is the sceptre over the kingdom of Christ. For the Lord loves righteousness and hates wickedness (Psalm 45:6-7). He will not tolerate evil among his people.

And a final word—as mentioned in chapter 4, it is the responsibility of parents to teach their children the moral law of God and the divine plan for sexual conduct from Scripture. The church should teach young people the meaning and purpose of marriage and the biblical virtues of chastity, modesty, self-control and faithfulness. The teaching of sex education, which comes from the mindset of the sexual revolutionaries, has no place in the Christian Church. There is no such thing as Christian sex education.

(Endnotes)

1 CARE, With CARE, leaflet.

2 CARE confidential, leaflet, Making a decision, available from website

3 ES Williams, W*hat is going on in Christian Crisis Pregnancy Counselling?* The Wakeman Trust and Belmont House Publishing, 2005, p48

4 *CARE Today*, Issue 10, Spring 2006, The grace call, pp6-7

5 Ibid.

6 ES Williams, *What is going on in Christian Crisis Pregnancy Counselling?* pp51-52

7 Ibid. p81

8 CARE's evaluate website, Student's page, It's Our Choice, www.evaluate.org.uk/Articles/160780/evaluate_informing_choice/Students/Its_Our_Choice.aspx

9 CARE's evaluate website, Teacher's page, Sex or no sex? that is the question! www.evaluate.org.uk/Groups/16674/evaluate_informing_choice/Teachers/Teachers.aspx

10 Sex Education Forum website, National Children's Bureau, 2008, We want more! Sex education charter: www.ncb.org.uk/sef

11 ES Williams, *Lessons in Depravity*, Belmont House Publishing, 2003, p290-91

Other publications by ES Williams on page 118

Other publications by ES Williams

The Great Divorce Controversy (2000)
The divorce issue is examined from the widest possible perspective, searching for the ideas and attitudes that underlie the move to mass divorce. Biblical teaching as it relates to marriage and divorce is outlined. The author concludes that the Christian Church needs to re-examine its teaching of marriage and divorce in the light of biblical truth.
Belmont House Publishing. Hard cover, pages 416, illustrations 22, index.
ISBN: 0 9529939 3 7

Lessons in Depravity – sex education and the sexual revolution (2003)
A devastating critique of sex education ideology. The history of sex education in the UK is outlined, and the link between the explicit messages of the sex educators and the ideology of the sexual revolution is documented. In view of the inherent moral dangers, parents cannot afford to stand back and leave the moral instruction of their children in the hands of State sex education.
Belmont House Publishing. Soft cover, 328 pages, 6 illustrations, index
ISBN: 0 9529939 5 3

What is going on in Christian Crisis Pregnancy Counselling? (2005)
The nondirective, options crisis pregnancy counselling provided by CARE's network of counselling centres is described and found to be no different from that provided by pro-abortion counselling services. The underlying philosophy of CARE's approach is based on situation ethics rather than biblical truth.
Wakeman Trust and Belmont House Publishing. Soft cover, 91 pages
ISBN: 1 870855 45 0

The Outrage of Amoral Sex Education (2006)
The amoral nature of the sex education that is taught in the school classroom is described in graphic detail.
Belmont House Publishing. Soft cover, 76 pages, 29 illustrations
ISBN: 0 9548493 0 2